First Steps in Music Theory

First Steps in Music Theory

Grades 1 to 5

Eric Taylor

ABRSM

First published in 1999 by The Associated Board of the Royal Schools of Music
(Publishing) Limited, a wholly owned subsidiary of ABRSM.

Reprinted in 2000, 2004, 2005, 2008, 2009, 2012, 2014, 2017

© 1999 by The Associated Board of the Royal Schools of Music

ISBN 978 1 86096 090 1

AB 2719

All rights reserved. No part of this publication may be reproduced, stored in a
retrieval system, or transmitted in any form or by any means, electronic,
mechanical, photocopying, recording, or otherwise, without the prior permission
of the copyright owner.

A CIP catalogue record for this book is available from The British Library.

Cover design by Adam Hay, London
Text design and setting by Geoffrey Wadsley
Music origination by Jack Thompson
Printed in England by Martins the Printers Ltd, Berwick upon Tweed,
on materials from sustainable sources

Contents

	Preface	xi

Grade 1

Section

1	Time Values: Crotchets, Minims and Semibreves	1
2	Bars and Time Signatures	1
3	Time Values: Quavers and Semiquavers	3
4	Letter Names of Notes	4
5	The Stave and Clefs	5
6	Writing on a Stave	6
7	Ledger Lines	7
8	Sharps, Flats and Naturals	8
9	Semitones, Tones, and the Scale of C Major	9
10	The Scales of G, D and F Major	10
11	Rests	12
12	Tied and Dotted Notes	13
13	Keys and Key Signatures	15
14	Accidentals	18
15	The Degrees of a Scale	19
16	Tonic Triads	21
17	Intervals (Number)	22
18	The Grouping of Notes Within a Bar	24
19	Performance Directions (Terms and Signs)	27

Grade 2

Section

1	Time Signatures: $\frac{2}{2}$, $\frac{3}{2}$, $\frac{4}{4}$ and $\frac{3}{8}$	29
2	Triplets	30
3	The Grouping of Notes	32
4	The Grouping of Rests	33
5	Ledger Lines	38
6	The Scale of A Major	38
7	The Scales of B Flat and E Flat Major	39
8	Key Signatures	41
9	Harmonic and Melodic Forms of the Minor Scale	42
10	The Harmonic Scales of A, E and D Minor	44
11	The Melodic Scales of A, E and D Minor	45
12	Relative Major and Minor Keys	47
13	Intervals	48
14	Performance Directions (Terms and Signs)	49

Grade 3

Section

1	Simple and Compound Time	53
2	The Grouping of Notes in $\frac{6}{8}$, $\frac{9}{8}$ and $\frac{12}{8}$	55
3	The Grouping of Rests in $\frac{6}{8}$, $\frac{9}{8}$ and $\frac{12}{8}$	57
4	Demisemiquaver Notes and Rests	61
5	Upbeat Starts	62
6	Ledger Lines and Octave Signs	65
7	Octave Transposition	66
8	The Major Scales of E and A Flat	68
9	The Minor Scales of B, F Sharp and C Sharp	69
10	The Minor Scales of G, C and F	71
11	Intervals	73
12	Performance Directions	76

Grade 4

Section

1	Breves	79
2	Double Dots	79
3	Regular Time Signatures	80
4	Duplets	82
5	Double Sharps and Flats; Enharmonic Equivalents	83
6	The Scales of B Major and G Sharp Minor	84
7	The Scales of D Flat Major and B Flat Minor	85
8	The Technical Names of Notes in Diatonic Scales	86
9	Intervals	88
10	Triads on the Tonic, Subdominant and Dominant	92
11	Chords on the Tonic, Subdominant and Dominant	95
12	The Chromatic Scale	97
13	Ornament Signs	99
14	The Alto Clef	101
15	General Questions	102

Grade 5

Section

1	Irregular Time Signatures	105
2	Irregular Time Divisions	106
3	The Tenor Clef; Octave Transpositions	107
4	The Scales of F Sharp Major and D Sharp Minor	109
5	The Scales of G Flat Major and E Flat Minor	111
6	Diatonic and Chromatic Intervals	112
7	Compound Intervals	114
8	Inversions of Triads	115
9	Identifying Chords	117
10	The $^6_4\,^5_3$ Progression	120
11	Chords at Cadence Points	122
12	Transposition by Instruments in B Flat, A and F	126
13	SATB in Short and Open Score	129
14	Ornaments	132
15	General Questions	138
	Index	143

Preface

Many teachers have said that it would be useful for students to have a grade-by-grade presentation of the basic facts of music theory, particularly one in a pocket-size format. *First Steps in Music Theory* has been written in response to this need.

First Steps in Music Theory is meant as a support for the other Associated Board theory publications — *The AB Guide to Music Theory* and Grades 1 to 5 of *Music Theory in Practice* — not as a substitute for them. It deals simply with things which must be *known*. Matters such as clefs, scales, key signatures, intervals, time values, time signatures, and the grouping of notes and rests need to be known and understood because they are essential elements of music. It is, of course, for this reason that the majority of questions in the Associated Board Grades 1 to 5 theory examinations deal with these elements. Questions which require greater musical creativity and insight, such as composing answering rhythms, recognising phrase patterns and setting words to music, are dealt with extensively at the appropriate places in *Music Theory in Practice* and are not covered here.

It is important to note how this book complements both *The AB Guide to Music Theory* and Grades 1 to 5 of *Music Theory in Practice*. Although *The AB Guide* includes all the information required for the Associated Board's theory examinations, it was not intended for examination candidates alone, and it is not broken up into grades. *Music Theory in Practice*, on the other hand, was specifically designed as a series of workbooks leading to the various grades of the theory examinations. It assumes that students will have studied the relevant sections of *The AB Guide*, and is mainly concerned with advice on how to set about answering the types of questions set in the examinations, and with providing exercises for practice.

First Steps in Music Theory will, I hope, prove to be invaluable to music students of all ages and abilities while fulfilling its primary function of providing support for the preparation of the first five grades of music theory examinations.

Eric Taylor

Grade 1

1 Time Values: Crotchets, Minims and Semibreves

People often tap their feet 'in time' when they are listening to a piece of music, especially if it is a march or a dance. They are tapping the steady **beats** of the music. In Grade 1, beats are shown like this: ♩ ♩ ♩ ♩ ♩ ♩ ♩ ♩ . These signs are called **crotchets** or 'quarter notes'. A slightly different sign, ♩ , is used for a sound which lasts as long as *two* crotchets. It is called a **minim** or 'half note'. A sound which lasts as long as *four* crotchets is written o : this is a **semibreve** or 'whole note'. Here crotchets, minims and semibreves are lined up together:

crotchets (quarter notes) ♩ ♩ ♩ ♩ ♩ ♩ ♩ ♩ ♩ ♩ ♩ ♩

minims (half notes) ♩   ♩   ♩   ♩   ♩   ♩

semibreves (whole notes) o   o   o

A semibreve lasts as long as two minims or four crotchets, or we can say that a semibreve has the same 'time value' as two minims or four crotchets. Therefore a minim has the same time value as two crotchets, but only half the time value of a semibreve.

2 Bars and Time Signatures

Beats in music form groups — most commonly, groups of two, three or four. The first beat in each group is felt to be a little stronger than the others. When they are written down, an upright line is placed at the end of each group:

The groups are **bars** or 'measures', and the upright lines are **bar lines**. Remember that it is the first beat in each bar, the beat *after* the bar line, which is felt to be a little stronger than the others.

At the beginning of a piece of music there is a **time signature**. In Grade 1, three time signatures are used: $\frac{2}{4}$, $\frac{3}{4}$ and $\frac{4}{4}$. In each case, the top figure shows *how many* beats there will be in a bar. The bottom figure shows *what kind* of beats they will be. Crotchet (quarter note) beats are shown by the figure 4, so:

$\frac{2}{4}$ means two crotchet beats in a bar

$\frac{3}{4}$ means three crotchet beats in a bar

$\frac{4}{4}$ means four crotchet beats in a bar

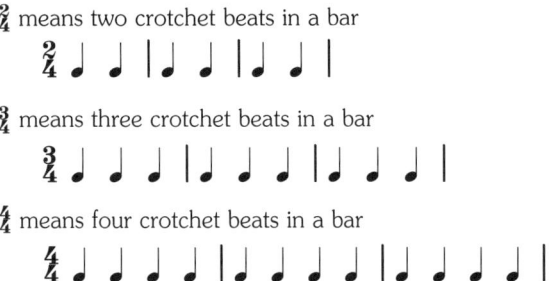

$\frac{4}{4}$ is often called 'common time', and instead of $\frac{4}{4}$ the sign **C** may be used. However, **C** is not a capital C: it is a sign which has survived from an early and different system of writing time signatures.[1]

---

[1] See *The AB Guide to Music Theory*, Part I, 1/2.

A bar may include notes longer or shorter than one-beat notes, provided they all add up to the number of beats given in the time signature. These bars use all the time values which we have seen so far:

3 Time Values: Quavers and Semiquavers

Grade 1 also uses time values shorter than crotchets. The **quaver** or 'eighth note', ♪, lasts only half the length of a crotchet. The **semiquaver** or 'sixteenth note', ♬, lasts only a quarter of the length of a crotchet. In other words, two quavers last as long as a crotchet, and so do four semiquavers.

A different way of writing quavers is normally used when there are two or more of them together in a bar. For example,

would usually be written

Semiquavers too may be written differently: for example,

$\frac{2}{4}$ ♩ ♬♬ may become $\frac{2}{4}$ ♩ ♬♬

Notes which are joined together in this way are said to be 'beamed' together. We shall go into more detail about this later on (see Section 18).

4 Letter Names of Notes

Music is made out of fixed sounds like those produced by the keys on a keyboard. Each key produces its own sound — a sound which is higher or lower than the sounds produced by any of the other keys — and it always produces the *same* sound. Different types of instrument produce their sounds in different ways but it is easiest to understand how musical notes are arranged and named by looking at a keyboard. This is because on a keyboard the keys produce notes in ascending order, starting with the lowest note on the left and finishing with the highest note on the right. The notes are named after the first seven letters of the alphabet: A, B, C, D, E, F and G. All keyboards have a mixture of black and white notes. The black notes are fitted in between the white notes, in alternate groups of two and three. A white note between the second and third of a group of three black notes is called A:

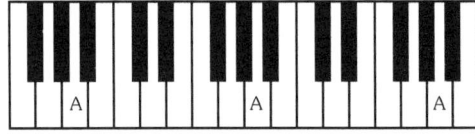

lower notes ←   → higher notes

The following white notes are B, C, D, E, F and G. After G we start again (A, B, C etc.):

5 The Stave and Clefs

When music is written down, these notes (A, B, C etc.) are shown on five lines called a **stave** or 'staff'. Each line or space represents one note:

Notice that when musicians say that a note is 'on' a line they mean that the line runs *through* it. The lines or spaces of a stave are counted from the bottom: 'the second line of the stave' is the second line from the bottom, and 'the fourth space' is the top space.

To show which note is A and which is B etc., a sign called a **clef** is placed at the beginning of each stave. In Grade 1 you will find only the two most common clefs: the **treble clef** 𝄞 for the higher notes, and the **bass clef** 𝄢 for lower notes. The treble clef is also called the 'G' clef because it curls around a line, the second line, which then represents the note G:

From this we can tell the names of the notes represented by all the lines and the spaces in a stave with the treble clef:

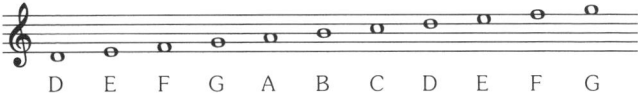

D   E   F   G   A   B   C   D   E   F   G

The bass clef is usually written 𝄢 (as shown above), but it can also be written 𝄷. Notice that both of these signs have two dots at the end. They go on either side of a line, the fourth line, which then represents the note F:

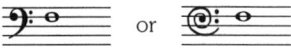

That is why the bass clef is also called the 'F' clef. Here are the names of all the notes represented by the lines and spaces in a stave with a bass clef:

F   G   A   B   C   D   E   F   G   A   B

6 Writing on a Stave

So far we have used only semibreves to show notes on a stave. The shorter notes (minims, crotchets etc.) all have a **note-head** (o or •) and a **stem** (|). Quavers and semiquavers also have **flags** at the end of their stems: one for quavers (♪) and two for semiquavers (♬). It is the note-head which goes on the line or in the space wanted:

Flags are sometimes called 'tails'.

If a note is below the middle line, the stem should go up on the *right*, like those in the example above. If it is above the middle line, the stem should go down — from the *left* of the note-head:

Notice also that when stems go down the flags still point to the right (𝅘𝅥𝅮 𝅘𝅥𝅮 , not), not). The stem of a note *on* the middle line can go up or down.

The time signature is put in at the beginning of the music, after the clef. The clef goes in again at the beginning of every new stave, but the time signature does not. Bar lines stretch across the stave from the top line to the bottom:

At the end of a piece there is always a double bar line:

7 Ledger Lines

Whichever clef is used, it is sometimes necessary to write notes higher or lower than those on the stave. When this happens, short extra lines are added below or above the stave:

These extra lines are called **ledger lines**. Notice that they are only long enough for the notes which need them, and that they are not joined together:

not

In Grade 1 the only ledger lines used are the one below a treble clef stave and the one above a bass clef stave:

Both of these notes are C. They are particularly important because they are both the *same* C, so we have two different ways of writing the same note. The C they both represent is the C nearest the middle of the keyboard on a piano. Because of this, it is always called **middle C**. Now we can put together all the white notes used in Grade 1, and see where they are on a keyboard:

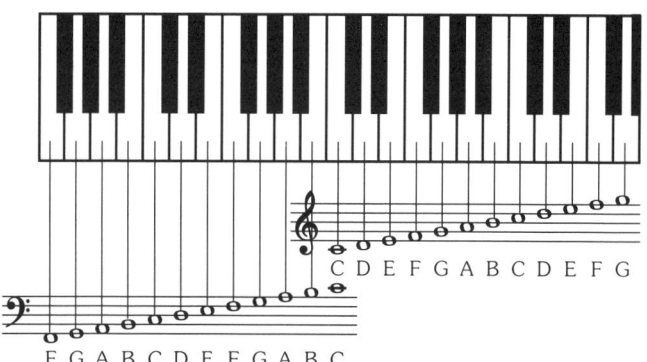

8 Sharps, Flats and Naturals

The black notes on a keyboard take their names from the white notes. A black note to the right of a white note has the same letter name but with 'sharp' added. The music sign for 'sharp' is ♯. The black note to the right of C is therefore C sharp (C♯), the black note to the right of D is D sharp (D♯), and so on:

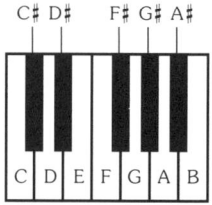

There is also another way of naming the black notes. A black note to the *left* of a white note has the same name as the white note but with 'flat' added. The music sign for 'flat' is ♭ (notice that it is not quite the same as the letter b). The black note to the left of D is therefore D flat (D♭), the black note to the left of E is E flat (E♭), and so on:

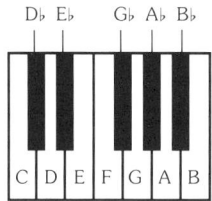

Although every black note can have two names, usually only one of them would be correct. We shall begin to see why this is so in Section 10.

A letter name by itself (e.g. 'C') is always understood to mean the white note, but if it is necessary to make quite sure that it is the white note which is meant, 'natural' is added. The music sign for 'natural' is ♮, so the full name of a white note C is C natural (C♮).

9 Semitones, Tones, and the Scale of C Major

The distance from one note to another is called the **interval** between them. The smallest interval on a keyboard is the one between any note and the note *immediately* next to it: this interval is a **semitone**. The interval between the white note B and the white note C is a semitone, and so is the interval between E♮ and F♮. All other semitones include a black note, for example C♮–C♯, C♯–D♮, D♮–D♯ (or D–E♭). Two semitones together make a **tone**, for example C♮–D♮, D♮–E♮, E♮–F♯.

If you play all the white notes from C to the next C to the right, one after the other, you will have played a **scale**:

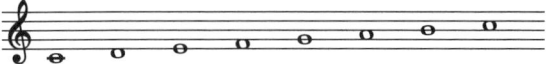

This particular scale is the scale of C major: 'C' because that is the note it begins and ends on, and 'major' because of the way its semitones and tones are arranged. Here is the same scale (C major) with the semitones marked ⌐ ¬:

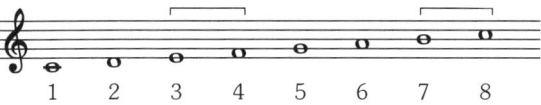

All the other intervals are tones.

10 The Scales of G, D and F Major

Two things about the C major scale above are very important and need to be remembered:
- Between the bottom and top notes there is a note on every line and in every space.
- There is a semitone between the 3rd and 4th notes, and another between the 7th and 8th notes; all the other intervals are tones.

These things are important because they are true of *all* major scales: they are what makes a scale 'major'. (There are also other types of scale, but the scales used in Grade 1 are all major.) So to write a major scale beginning on, say, G, we start by writing a note on every line and in every space between the two Gs:

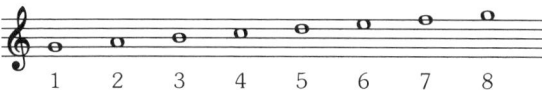

Then we check the intervals. All the intervals are correct, including the semitone between the 3rd and 4th notes (B and C), until we get to the last two notes: F and G. Here the interval between the 6th and 7th notes (E–F) is a semitone, and the interval between the 7th and 8th notes (F–G) is a tone. This is wrong: the semitone is in the wrong place. The interval between the 6th and 7th notes should be a tone, and the interval between the 7th and 8th notes should be a semitone. But it is easy to put matters right. All that is needed is to raise the 7th note a semitone — in other words, to change the F to F♯:

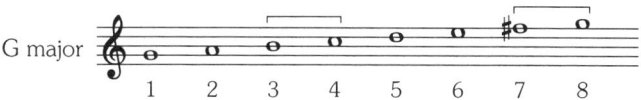

Notice that F♯ cannot be written as G♭ because there would then be a gap in the scale, with no note on the top line:

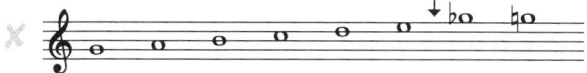

Every major scale except C needs at least one black note on the keyboard. If we try to write a major scale beginning on D, we shall find that we need two: to keep the correct pattern of semitones and tones we shall need to raise ('sharpen') not only the 7th note but also the 3rd:

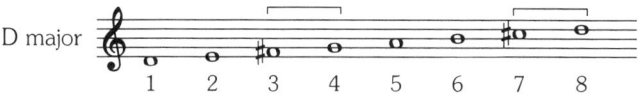

Sometimes it is necessary to lower ('flatten') one or more notes in order to keep the correct pattern. In Grade 1 there is only one example, the scale of F major, in which the 4th note, B, has to be changed to B♭:

F major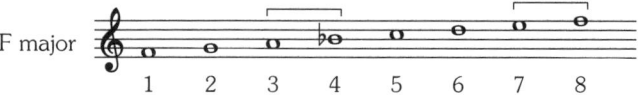

There is more about these scales in Section 13.

11 Rests

Moments of silence in music have to be measured exactly, just as the sounds do. Signs which show the length of silences are called **rests**. And just as there are signs showing the time values of notes, so there are signs showing the time values of rests. Those used in Grade 1 are set out here side by side:

	Notes	Rests
semibreve or whole note	𝅝	𝄻
minim or half note	𝅗𝅥	𝄼
crotchet or quarter note	𝅘𝅥	𝄽 or ՝
quaver or eighth note	𝅘𝅥𝅮	𝄾
semiquaver or sixteenth note	𝅘𝅥𝅯	𝄿

The semibreve and minim rests look nearly the same, but the semibreve rest hangs *underneath* a line and the minim rest sits *on top* of a line. Normally, the semibreve rest hangs underneath the fourth line of a stave

and the minim rest sits on top of the middle line

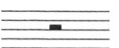

The other rests are placed like this (unless there is a reason why they should be higher or lower[2]):

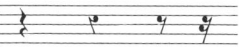

Although the crotchet rest can be written in either of two ways, 𝄽 is the standard form used in printed music, including examination papers.

A bar which is completely silent is marked with a semibreve rest — not only in $\frac{4}{4}$ but also in $\frac{2}{4}$ and $\frac{3}{4}$.

12 Tied and Dotted Notes

A **tie** (⌒ or ⌣) joins notes which are next to each other and which have the same **pitch**, meaning that one note must not be higher or lower than another. Tied notes become one continuous sound, their time values being added together. For example,

sounds the same as

---

[2] See *The AB Guide to Music Theory*, Part I, 3/1.

Notice that a tie goes from the head of the first note to the head of the next, on the outside:

Any number of notes can be joined in this way, provided they are next to each other and have the same pitch. (There is more about ties in Section 18.)

A **dot** after a note makes it longer by half its value:

$$\text{\musicnote}$$

So there are two ways of making a note longer: it can be tied or it can be dotted. For example:

However, you cannot always choose which to use. One important difference between them is that a tie can be used across a bar line, e.g.

but a dot cannot.

If the note is in a space, the dot goes in the same space (as in the examples above). If the note is on a line, the dot normally goes in the space above:

13 Keys and Key Signatures

A piece of music made from the notes of a scale is said to be in the **key** of that scale, and the first note of the scale is the **keynote** of the music. This, for instance, is in the key of D major because it uses the notes of the scale of D major:

Usually, however, the necessary sharps or flats are not put in individually before all the notes which need them. Instead, they are shown at the beginning of each line of the music, after the clef. This makes the music easier to read. The above melody, for example, would normally be written like this:

Sharp or flat signs after the clef are the **key signature** of the music. In the example above, notice that only one F has been marked with a ♯ in the key signature: the one on the top line. Also, only one C has been marked with a ♯: the one in the third space. This is because a sharp or a flat in a key signature always applies to *all* notes with the same letter name; so all three Fs in the melody are to become F♯, and both the Cs are to become C♯.

The music examples printed on the next two pages show all the scales set for Grade 1. They are printed here in semibreves, both going up (ascending) and coming down (descending), and in both the treble and the bass clefs. The semitones are marked ⌐⎯⎯⌐. There are no sharps or flats in the first scale, C major, and therefore it has no key signature. The other scales are printed both without and with key signatures.

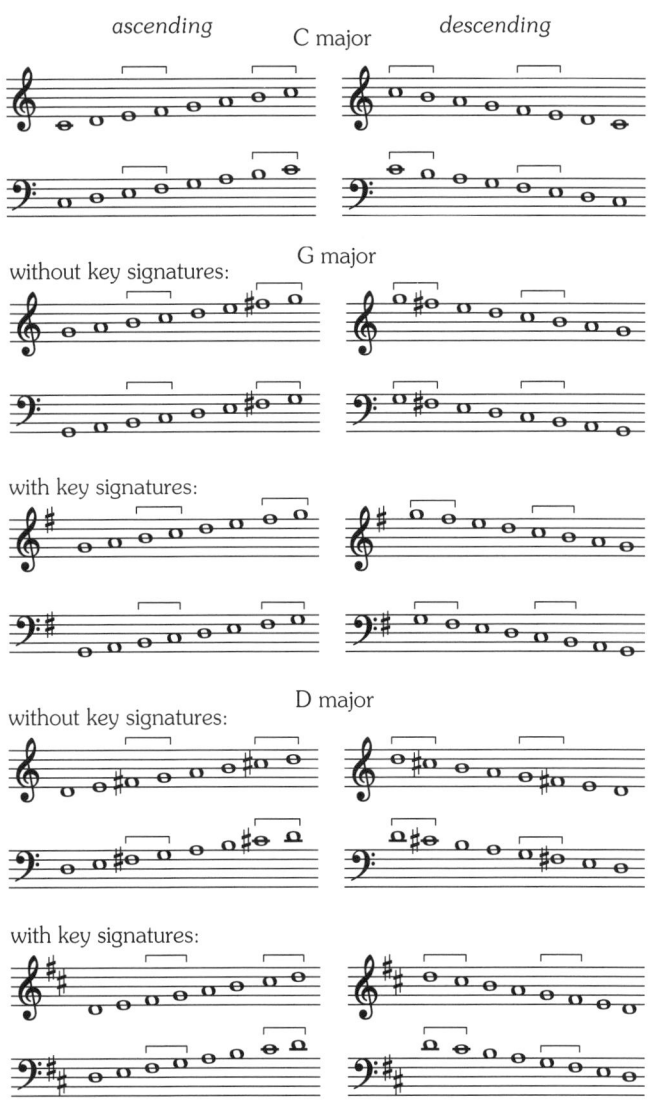

F major

without key signatures:

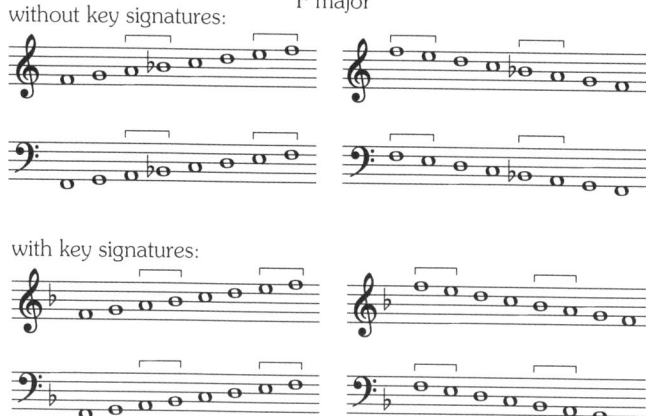

with key signatures:

Note carefully how the key signatures were arranged above: the sharps and flats must always be on exactly the right lines or in the right spaces according to the clef:

G major (one sharp: F♯)

D major (two sharps: F♯ and C♯)

F major (one flat: B♭)

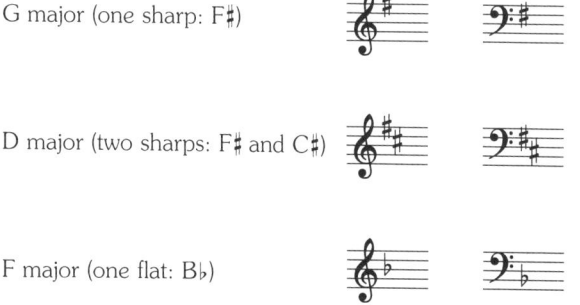

14 Accidentals

Individual notes can be raised or lowered a semitone by using a sharp, flat or natural sign. For example, the second note here is F sharp (because of the key signature), but the ♮ in front of the last note in bar 1 changes the note to F *natural*:

Similarly, in bar 1 both the Gs are G naturals, but in bar 2 the ♯ sign raises the first G to G *sharp*. The ♮ sign then changes the last G back to G *natural* again: in other words, the ♮ 'cancels' the ♯. Sharps, flats and naturals such as these are called **accidentals**.

An accidental also applies to all repetitions of the note in the same bar:

or until it is replaced by another accidental:

Thus these flats marked * are unnecessary, and should be regarded as incorrect:

Unlike a sharp or a flat in a key signature, however, an accidental applies only to notes on the *same line* or in the *same space*. Therefore the top G here is G natural, in spite of the ♯ before the second note:

(G♯)   (G♮)

An accidental stays in force throughout a note tied over a bar line:

   not

(E♭ ——)

But if the same accidental is required again after the tied note, it must be written in again. The ♯ marked * here is an example:

15 The Degrees of a Scale

The various notes of a scale (1st, 2nd, 3rd etc.) are also known as **degrees** of the scale: the 1st note is the 1st degree, the 2nd note is the 2nd degree, and so on. Therefore we can say that every major scale has a semitone between the 3rd and 4th degrees of the scale, and between the 7th and 8th degrees. For example:

in D major (ascending)

in D major (descending)

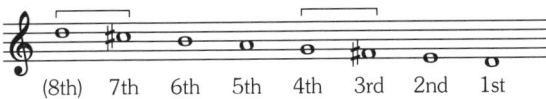

in F major (descending)

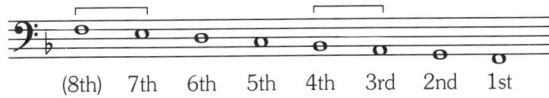

Note that in descending scales, we still count the degrees from the bottom up. Normally, however, the term '8th degree' is not used, because the '8th' degree has the same letter name as the 1st degree. So the top note of the scale is the 1st degree again, as in these examples:

D major (ascending)

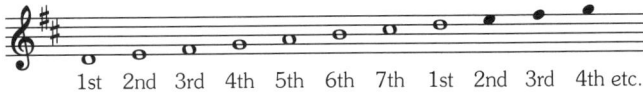

C major (descending)

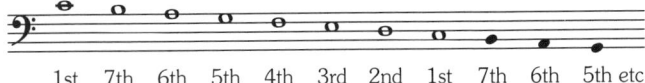

(The black note-heads show how the numbering continues if the scale goes on further.)

The next example is the same as the melody printed on p. 15, but with the degree of the scale added underneath each note:

3rd   1st 2nd   5th 6th 7th 1st 3rd   2nd 3rd 4th 5th 7th   1st

16 Tonic Triads

As well as numbers, the various degrees of a scale also have names. In Grade 1, the only one you will need to know is the name of the 1st degree, which is called the **tonic**. When the 1st, 3rd and 5th degrees of a major scale are played together they are called a **tonic triad**. All of these, for example, are tonic triads in the key of C major:

Below are the tonic triads of all the other Grade 1 keys in the treble and bass clefs, printed with their key signatures. The bottom note of each triad is the keynote:

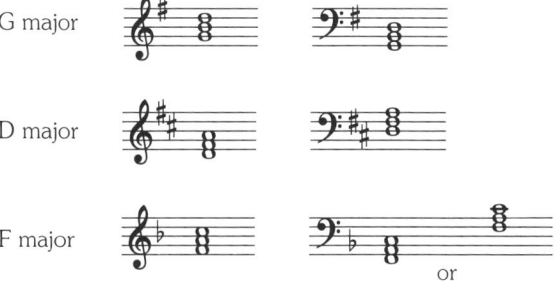

If the tonic triad of D major is written *without* a key signature it will of course need an accidental — a ♯ before the F:

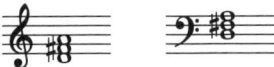

17 Intervals (Number)

'Semitone' and 'tone' are words which apply only to notes which are next to each other on the keyboard, or next-but-one. But intervals can also be described as numbers, and in this way you can describe the interval between *any* two notes. The 'number' of an interval is the number of scale-degrees which it contains or, to put it another way, the number of letter names which are included in it. For example:

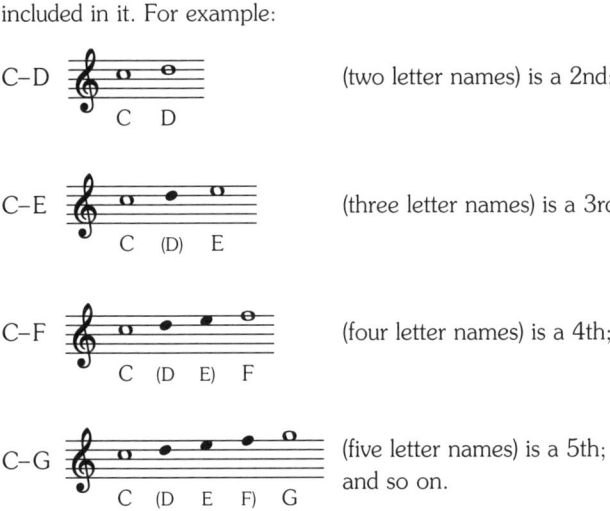

In Grade 1, the lower note of an interval will always be the keynote of one of your scales (C, G, D, F). So if the upper note is, say, the 5th degree of the scale, the interval also will be a 5th. You will only be asked about intervals up to an 8th. The 8th itself is called an **octave** (written as '8ve'). These are examples of all the Grade 1 intervals, shown here in the treble clef:

C major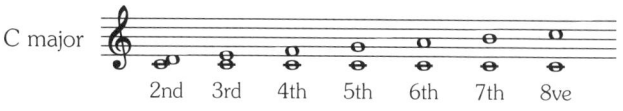

G major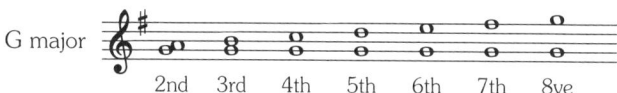

D major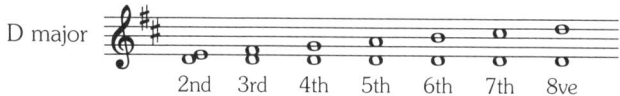

F major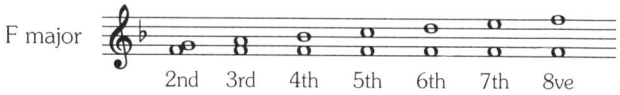

If the two notes of an interval are played together (as above) it is a 'harmonic' interval. If they are played one after the other, e.g.

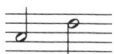

it is a 'melodic' interval.

18 The Grouping of Notes Within a Bar

There are some conventions about the ways in which notes are grouped together. They help the performer to read the music more easily and quickly. Below are some which you may need to remember in Grade 1, particularly when you write the answering two-bar rhythm.

1 Beam together
(a) two quavers which could be replaced by a crotchet:

(b) four quavers which could be replaced by a minim:

(c) six quavers filling a complete bar of 3/4:

(d) four semiquavers which could be replaced by a crotchet:

(e) and these groups which could be replaced by a crotchet:

(Notice how single semiquavers are beamed: ♪♪ ♪ , for example, becomes ♬ ♩)

There is an important exception to (b): in 4/4 do not beam quavers across the middle of a bar (between the 2nd and 3rd beats):

4/4 ♩ ♫♫♫♫ ♩ | is wrong;

4/4 ♩ ♫♫ ♫♫ ♩ | is right.

2 Avoid ties where possible

Do not write tied notes within a bar if you can use a single note (or a dotted note) instead. So write:

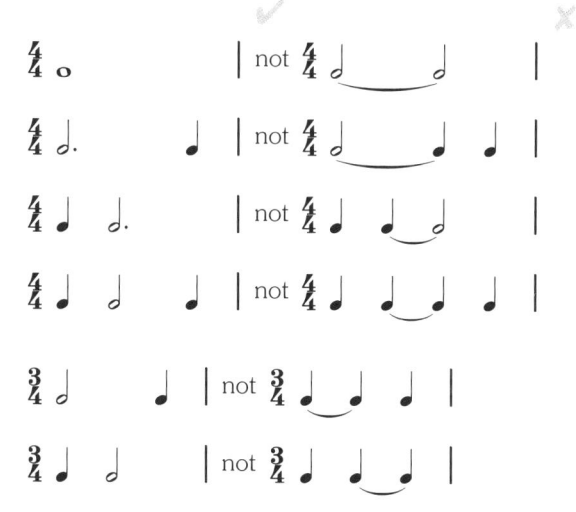

4/4 o | not 4/4 ♩—♩ |

4/4 ♩. ♩ | not 4/4 ♩—♩ ♩ |

4/4 ♩ ♩. | not 4/4 ♩ ♩—♩ |

4/4 ♩ ♩ ♩ | not 4/4 ♩ ♩—♩ ♩ |

3/4 ♩ ♩ | not 3/4 ♩ ♩—♩ |

3/4 ♩ ♩ | not 3/4 ♩ ♩—♩ |

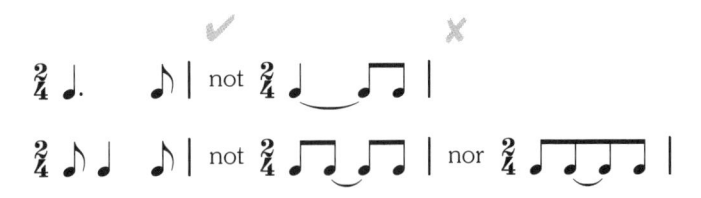

[musical examples showing correct and incorrect beaming in 2/4 time]

However, a tie *must* be used between beats if one of the notes is a semiquaver. For example, write:

[musical example]

3 Choices

Two or more groups of beamed notes may often be beamed together. For example,

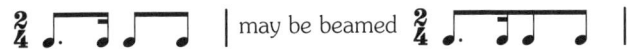

[musical example] may be beamed [musical example]

Both of these are clear, and therefore acceptable: it is not the case that one is 'right' and the other 'wrong'. On the other hand, these two groups of beamed notes

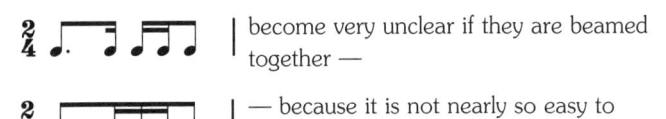

[musical example] become very unclear if they are beamed together —

[musical example] — because it is not nearly so easy to see where the second beat begins.

This last example, therefore, is unsatisfactory.

Sometimes you may notice in your music a place where a convention is broken. If this happens, a likely explanation could be that the composer is indicating something special about the way in which the music is to be played.[3]

---

[3] For more information see *The AB Guide to Music Theory*, Part I, 5/1, 6/1, 6/3, 11/2.

19 Performance Directions (Terms and Signs)

Below is a list of Italian words and their meanings which you should know in Grade 1. (It is the same as the list printed in *Music Theory in Practice*, Grade 1.)

accelerando (or *accel.*)	gradually getting quicker
adagio	slow
allegretto	fairly quick (but not as quick as *allegro*)
allegro	quick (literally 'cheerful')
andante	at a medium ('walking') speed
cantabile	in a singing style
crescendo (or *cresc.*)	gradually getting louder
da capo (or *D.C.*)	repeat from the beginning
dal segno (or *D.S.*)	repeat from the sign 𝄋
decrescendo (or *decresc.*)	gradually getting quieter
diminuendo (or *dim.*)	gradually getting quieter
fine	the end
f (= *forte*)	loud
ff (= *fortissimo*)	very loud
legato	smoothly
lento	slow
mezzo	half
mf (= *mezzo forte*)	moderately loud (literally 'half' loud)
mp (= *mezzo piano*)	moderately quiet (literally 'half' quiet)
moderato	moderately (*allegro moderato*: moderately quick)
p (= *piano*)	quiet
pp (= *pianissimo*)	very quiet
poco	a little
rallentando (or *rall.*)	gradually getting slower

ritardando (or *ritard.* or *rit.*)	gradually getting slower
ritenuto (or *riten.* or *rit.*)	held back
staccato (or *stacc.*)	detached
tempo	speed, time (*a tempo*: in time)

You should also know these signs, printed in *Music Theory in Practice*, Grade 1:

———◁	= *crescendo* (gradually getting louder)
▷———	= *diminuendo* (gradually getting quieter)
⌒	over two *different* notes (not to be confused with a tie) or over a group of notes is called a 'slur': perform the notes smoothly
8va	= *ottava* (octave)
8va ⎤ *8* ⎤	(over a note or notes): perform an octave higher
8va ⎦ *8* ⎦	(under a note or notes): perform an octave lower
.	a dot over or under a note ♩̇ = *staccato*
>	over or under a note ♩̇ = accent the note
⌒ over a note or rest ⌣ under a note or rest	pause on the note or rest
𝄇 and 𝄆	repeat marks — at the second sign, go back to the first sign and repeat the music from there (the first sign is left out if the music is repeated from the beginning)
M.M. ♩ = 72 (or just ♩ = 72)	72 crotchet beats in a minute (M.M. is short for Maelzel's Metronome)

Grade 2

1 Time Signatures: $\frac{2}{2}$, $\frac{3}{2}$, $\frac{4}{2}$ and $\frac{3}{8}$

The time signatures in Grade 1 all had **4** as their lower figure: $\frac{2}{4}$, $\frac{3}{4}$ and $\frac{4}{4}$. Grade 2 adds some time signatures with **2** or **8** as the lower figure: $\frac{2}{2}$, $\frac{3}{2}$, $\frac{4}{2}$ and $\frac{3}{8}$. The **2** shows that the beats are written as minims (half notes), and the **8** shows that the beats are written as quavers (eighth notes). So:

$\frac{2}{2}$ means two minim beats in a bar

$\frac{3}{2}$ means three minim beats in a bar

$\frac{4}{2}$ means four minim beats in a bar

$\frac{3}{8}$ means three quaver beats in a bar

On paper, music in $\frac{4}{4}$ looks exactly the same as music in $\frac{2}{2}$ if you ignore their time signatures. For example, this could be in either $\frac{4}{4}$ or $\frac{2}{2}$:

If there is a time signature of $\frac{4}{4}$, the music will be felt to have four beats in a bar, as marked ↑ here:

↑ ↑ ↑ ↑   ↑ ↑ ↑ ↑   ↑ ↑   ↑ ↑ ↑ ↑

But if there is a time signature of $\frac{2}{2}$ it will be felt to have two beats in a bar:

↑   ↑   ↑   ↑   ↑   ↑   ↑ ↑

Music with two beats in a bar is said to be in **duple** time. Music with three beats in a bar is in **triple** time, and music with four beats is in **quadruple time**. Therefore in Grade 2:

- the duple time signatures are $\frac{2}{4}$ and $\frac{2}{2}$;
- the triple time signatures are $\frac{3}{8}$, $\frac{3}{4}$ and $\frac{3}{2}$;
- the quadruple time signatures are $\frac{4}{4}$ and $\frac{4}{2}$.

2 Triplets

A **triplet** is a group of three notes performed in the time of two. For example:

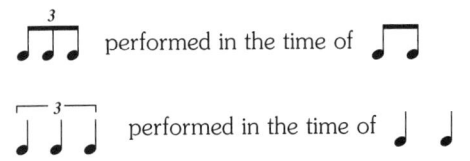

♪♪♪ (3) performed in the time of ♩♪

♩♩♩ (3) performed in the time of ♩ ♩

The sign for a triplet is the figure **3** written either above or below the middle note. A curved line (like a slur) or a square bracket may be added. This is not really necessary if the notes are beamed together, but it is usual in all other circumstances:

These are examples of minims and semiquavers forming triplet groups:

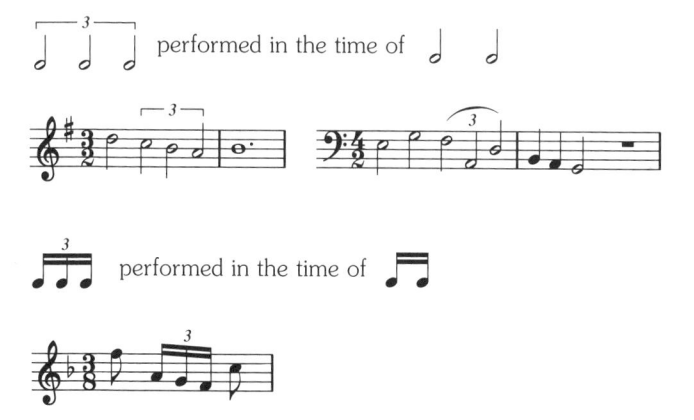

performed in the time of

performed in the time of

A triplet group can include rests, as can be seen in Section 3. It can also include notes with different values provided they add up to the equivalent of three equal notes:

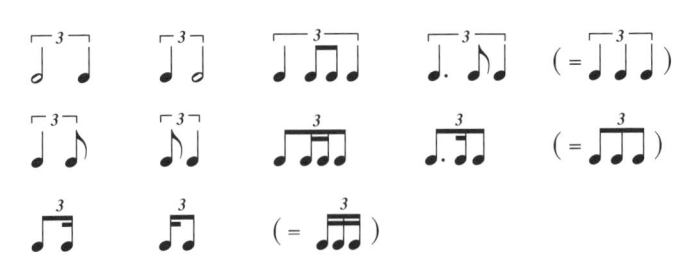

3 The Grouping of Notes

There are only a few points to add to what was said in Grade 1 about avoiding ties and about beaming notes:

1 Avoid ties where possible

In $\frac{3}{2}$ and $\frac{4}{2}$, write o· not o⌣d nor d⌣o

2 Beam together
(a) in $\frac{3}{8}$, six semiquavers filling a complete bar of $\frac{3}{8}$:

(b) in $\frac{2}{2}$, $\frac{3}{2}$ and $\frac{4}{2}$, eight semiquavers which could be replaced by a minim:

Compare the last example with:

The explanation for the different beaming is that in both

examples the notes are beamed in *beats*: two minim beats in $\frac{2}{2}$, and four crotchet beats in $\frac{4}{4}$.

Rests may be included amongst groups of notes which are beamed together:

4 The Grouping of Rests

In $\frac{2}{2}$, $\frac{3}{2}$ and $\frac{3}{8}$, a completely silent bar is shown by a semibreve rest:[1]

When bars contain both notes and rests, it is a general rule that a new rest should be used at the start of every silent beat:

with crotchet beats:

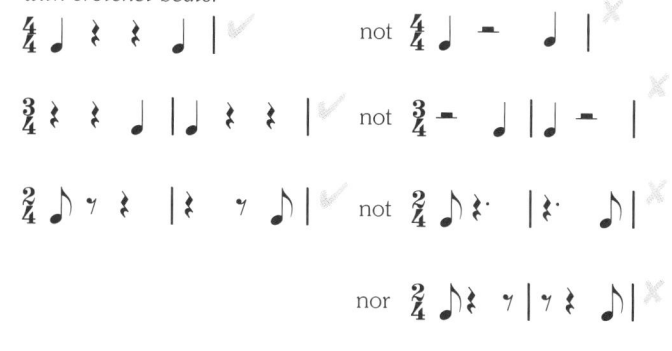

---

[1] The same is true of *all* time signatures except $\frac{4}{2}$, which requires a breve rest. However, you will not be asked about this in Grade 2. (Questions involving the use of breve notes and rests are not set until Grade 4.)

with quaver beats:

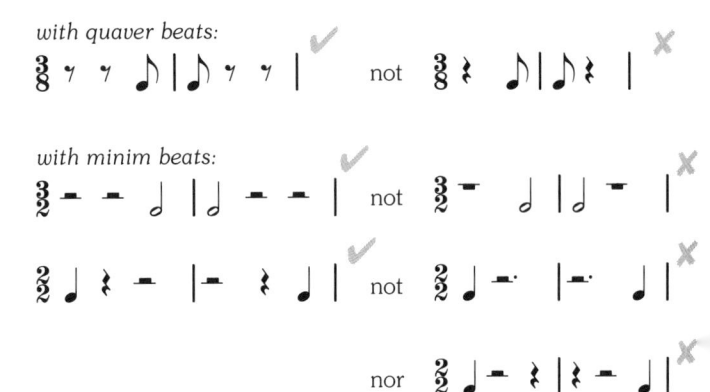

$\frac{3}{8}$ 𝄾 𝄾 ♪ | ♪ 𝄾 𝄾 | ✓ not $\frac{3}{8}$ 𝄾 ♪ | ♪ 𝄾 | ✗

with minim beats:

$\frac{3}{2}$ − − 𝅗𝅥 | 𝅗𝅥 − − | ✓ not $\frac{3}{2}$ − 𝅗𝅥 | 𝅗𝅥 − | ✗

$\frac{3}{2}$ 𝅗𝅥 𝄽 − | − 𝄽 𝅗𝅥 | ✓ not $\frac{3}{2}$ 𝅗𝅥 −. | −. 𝅗𝅥 | ✗

nor $\frac{3}{2}$ 𝅗𝅥 − 𝄽 | 𝄽 − 𝅗𝅥 | ✗

But otherwise there should be as few rests as possible:

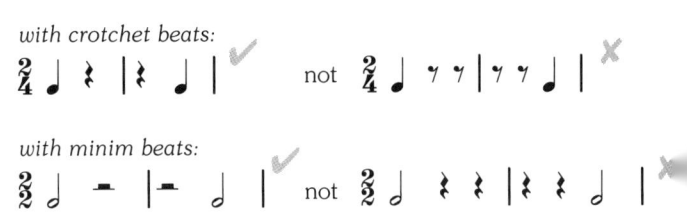

with crotchet beats:

$\frac{2}{4}$ 𝅘𝅥 𝄽 | 𝄽 𝅘𝅥 | ✓ not $\frac{2}{4}$ 𝅘𝅥 𝄾 𝄾 | 𝄾 𝄾 𝅘𝅥 | ✗

with minim beats:

$\frac{3}{2}$ 𝅗𝅥 − | − 𝅗𝅥 | ✓ not $\frac{3}{2}$ 𝅗𝅥 𝄽 𝄽 | 𝄽 𝄽 𝅗𝅥 | ✗

There is an important exception to the rule that 'a new rest should be used at the start of every silent beat'. When there are four beats in a bar, a two-beat rest should be used for the first two beats, or for the last two, but not in the middle:

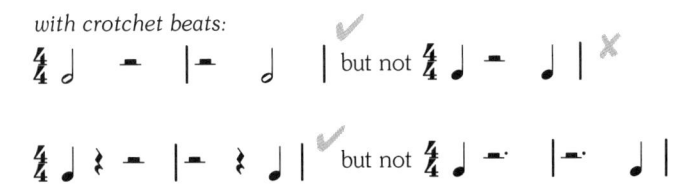

with crotchet beats:

$\frac{4}{4}$ 𝅘𝅥 − | − 𝅘𝅥 | ✓ but not $\frac{4}{4}$ 𝅘𝅥 − 𝅘𝅥 | ✗

$\frac{4}{4}$ 𝅘𝅥 𝄽 − | − 𝄽 𝅘𝅥 | ✓ but not $\frac{4}{4}$ 𝅘𝅥 −. | −. 𝅘𝅥 |

with minim beats:

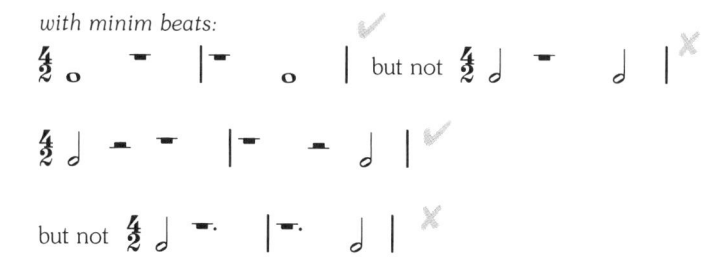

$\frac{4}{2}$ o — | — o | but not $\frac{4}{2}$ ♩ — ♩ |

$\frac{4}{2}$ ♩ — — | — — ♩ |

but not $\frac{4}{2}$ ♩ —. | —. ♩ |

Notice that two-beat *rests* in the middle of a four-beat bar are treated differently from two-beat *notes*:

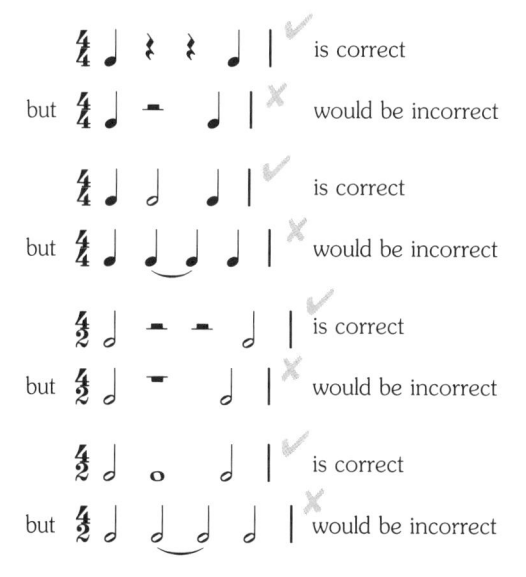

$\frac{4}{4}$ ♩ 𝄽 𝄽 ♩ | is correct

but $\frac{4}{4}$ ♩ — ♩ | would be incorrect

$\frac{4}{4}$ ♩ ♩ ♩ | is correct

but $\frac{4}{4}$ ♩ ♩‿♩ ♩ | would be incorrect

$\frac{4}{2}$ ♩ — — ♩ | is correct

but $\frac{4}{2}$ ♩ — ♩ | would be incorrect

$\frac{4}{2}$ ♩ o ♩ | is correct

but $\frac{4}{2}$ ♩ ♩‿♩ ♩ | would be incorrect

When a silence lasts for *less* than a full beat, each *subdivision* of the beat must start with a new rest. Here, 'subdivision' of the beat means each half beat or even each quarter beat. Below are examples of half-beat rests. To make them clearer, the full beats are marked ⌐ ⌐.

a ♩ beat can be divided into ♩ 𝄾 or 𝄾 ♩ :

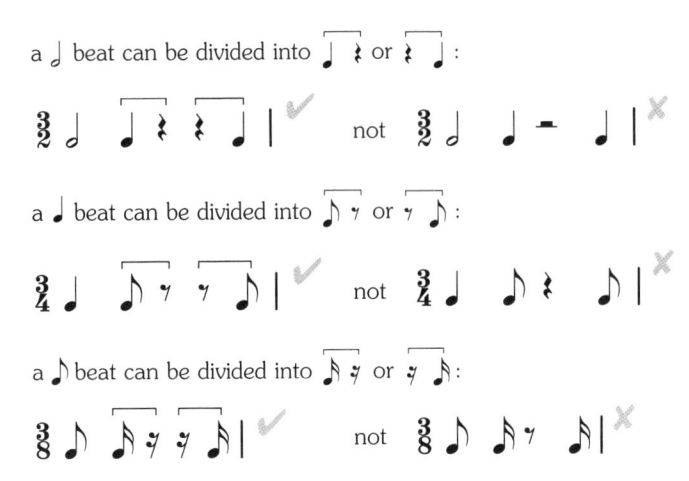

$\frac{3}{2}$ 𝅗𝅥 ♩ 𝄾 𝄾 ♩ | ✓   not $\frac{3}{2}$ 𝅗𝅥 ♩ — ♩ | ✗

a ♩. beat can be divided into ♪ 𝄾 or 𝄾 ♪ :

$\frac{3}{4}$ ♩. ♪ 𝄾 𝄾 ♪ | ✓   not $\frac{3}{4}$ ♩. ♪ 𝄾 ♪ | ✗

a ♪ beat can be divided into ♬ 𝄾 or 𝄾 ♬ :

$\frac{3}{8}$ ♪ ♬ 𝄾 𝄾 ♬ | ✓   not $\frac{3}{8}$ ♪ ♬ ♬ | ✗

A silence which lasts for *more* than a number of full beats is shown by as few rests as possible, but they still follow the rules explained above. The best way of understanding this is to see how the beats are arranged in a bar which contains only a single note, either at the end or at the beginning of the bar. For example, in a bar of $\frac{4}{4}$ ending with a semiquaver:

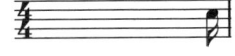

the rests are arranged

first,   a minim rest (for the first two crotchet beats);
second, a crotchet rest (for the third crotchet beat);
third,   a quaver rest (for the first half of the fourth crotchet beat);
last,   a semiquaver rest (to make up the second half of the beat).

(Notice that it is *not* standard practice to write the bar as

[musical notation: 4/4 bar with dotted minim rest and dotted quaver rest]

even though you may sometimes see this, and it is certainly simpler.)

If a bar of 4/4 *starts* with a semiquaver, the same rests are used to complete the bar, but they have to be arranged in reverse order:

[musical notation: 4/4 bar starting with semiquaver followed by semiquaver rest, quaver rest, crotchet rest, minim rest]

- the semiquaver rest completes the first (quaver) subdivision of the first beat;
- the quaver rest provides the second (quaver) subdivision of the first beat;
- the crotchet rest completes the first half of the bar;
- the minim rest provides the second half of the bar.

The rests are arranged the same way in 3/4, except that the minim rests become crotchet rests:

[musical notation: two 3/4 bars illustrating rest arrangements]

In 3/2 and 4/2, of course, the beat is a *minim*. The subdivisions of the minim beat at the end/beginning of a bar are shown by the brackets above these examples:

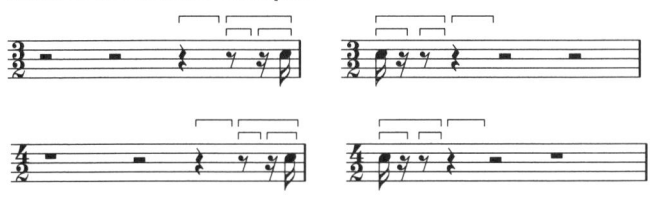

[musical notation: four examples in 3/2 and 4/2 with bracketed subdivisions]

In 2/2 the notes and rests would be exactly the same as in the 4/4 examples.

5 Ledger Lines

You may be asked to name or write notes needing up to two ledger lines above or below the stave. Below is the complete range of the Grade 2 notes. The new notes are written as black note-heads:

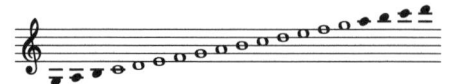

B C D E F G A B C D E F G A B C D E F G A B C D E F G A B C D

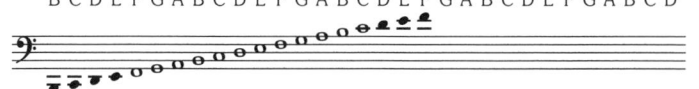

As you can see, some of these notes can be written either in the treble clef or in the bass clef. These two passages sound exactly the same:

6 The Scale of A Major

Remember that in every major scale there is a semitone between the 3rd and 4th degrees, and another between the 7th and 8th (=1st) degrees. All the other intervals are tones. So if we start a major scale on A, the notes C, F and G all have to become C♯, F♯ and G♯:

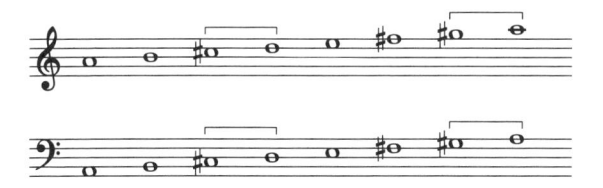

These three sharps form the key signature of A major:

When the scale is written with its key signature, the sharps are, of course, not needed before the individual notes:

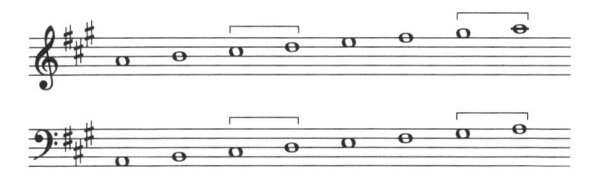

7 The Scales of B Flat and E Flat Major

All the scales we have had so far started on a white note of the keyboard. But these two scales — B♭ and E♭ major — both start on a black note. This is the scale of B♭ major:

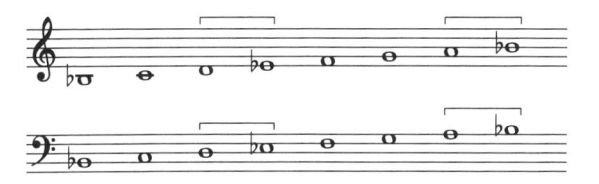

Notice that it needs an E♭ as well as the B♭ to keep the semitones in the right places. These two flats form the key signature of B♭ major:

Here is the scale of B♭ major written with its key signature:

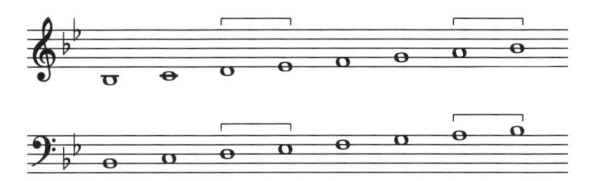

The scale of E♭ major needs an A♭ as well as B♭ and E♭:

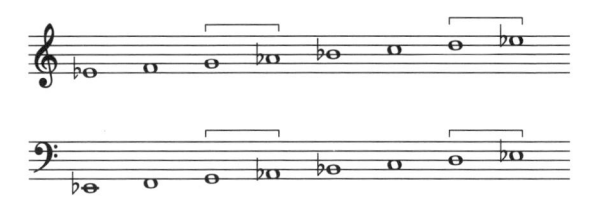

The three flats form the key signature of E♭ major:

Here is the descending scale of E♭ major written with its key signature:

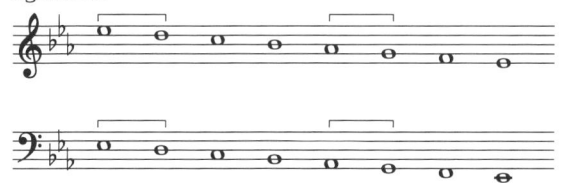

8 Key Signatures

The key signatures of the major scales in Grade 2 contain up to three sharps or up to three flats. Key signatures never mix sharps and flats: they contain *either* sharps *or* flats. Every new key signature adds one more sharp (or one more flat):

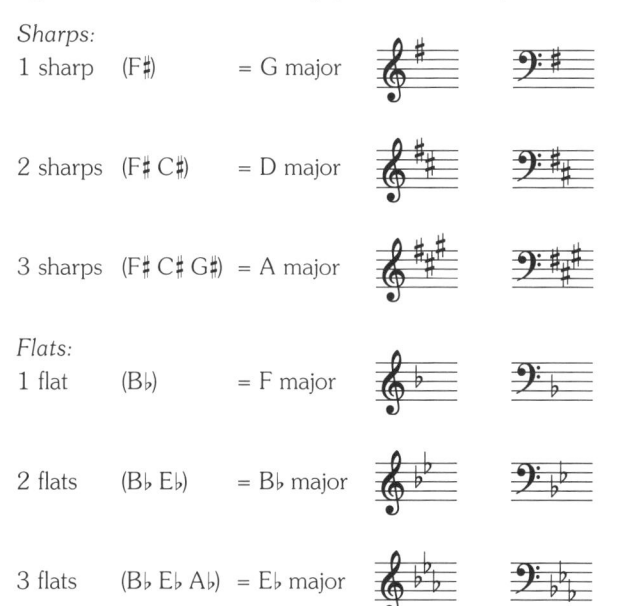

Sharps:
1 sharp   (F♯)   = G major

2 sharps (F♯ C♯)   = D major

3 sharps (F♯ C♯ G♯)   = A major

Flats:
1 flat   (B♭)   = F major

2 flats   (B♭ E♭)   = B♭ major

3 flats   (B♭ E♭ A♭)   = E♭ major

The sharps or flats in a key signature are always written in the order shown above. In the key of A major, for instance, the F♯ is written first, then the C♯, and lastly the G♯. Notice, too, where the sharps or flats are placed on the stave. Any other arrangement would be incorrect. (Here are some WRONG ways of writing these key signatures —

— but there are plenty more!)

9 Harmonic and Melodic Forms of the Minor Scale

As well as the major scale there is another type of scale with seven notes: the **minor** scale. But unlike the major scale, the minor scale exists in two different forms. These are the **harmonic minor scale** and the **melodic minor scale**.

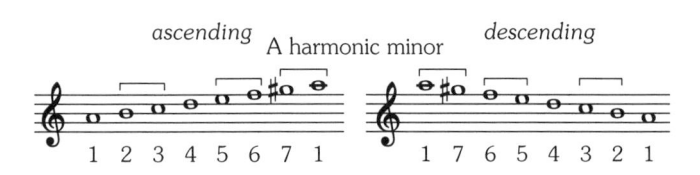

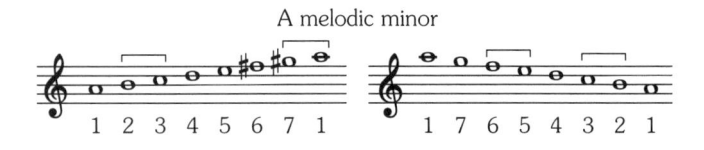

To illustrate the similarities and differences between harmonic and melodic minor scales, here is the scale of A minor in both forms. The semitones are marked ⌐⎯⎯⌐ , and the degrees of the scale are shown underneath.

Notice that:
- there is *always* a semitone between the 2nd and 3rd degrees of the scale;
- the harmonic minor scale (like the major scale) is the same both ascending and descending;
- the melodic minor scale is *not* the same coming down as going up. In the ascending scale the 6th and 7th degrees are raised by a sharp (F♯ and G♯), but in the descending scale the 7th and 6th degrees are unaltered (the notes are G natural and F natural);
- the harmonic minor scale includes three intervals of a semitone, and it also has an extra-wide interval (equal to three semitones) between the 6th and 7th degrees.

The good news is that in Grade 2 you will not be expected to know about *both* forms of the minor scales. You may choose which form you want to answer questions on — either harmonic or melodic. But you must know *which* form you are using; and you must stick to your chosen form, not chop and change between the two. The minor scales for this Grade are set out in full in the next two Sections. The harmonic scales are in Section 10 and the melodic scales in Section 11, so you will need to study only *one* of these sections.

In both sections the scales are printed without and with their key signatures except for the scale of A minor, which has no key signature (like the scale of C major). The A minor scales are given only in the bass clef since we have already had them in the treble clef.

10 The Harmonic Scales of A, E and D Minor

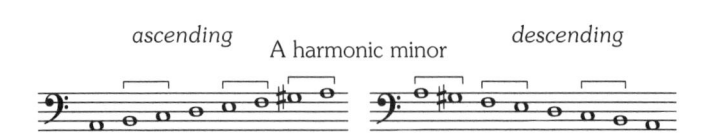

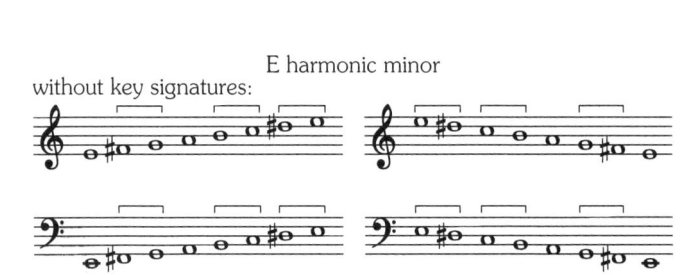

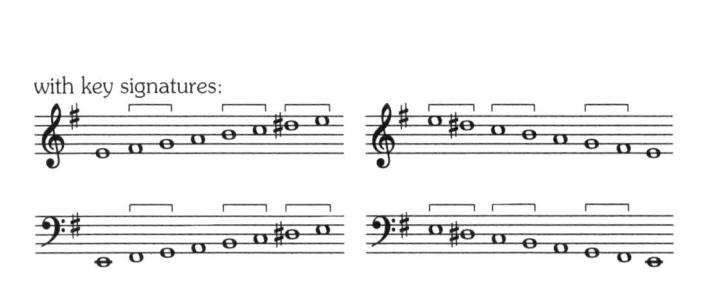

ascending A harmonic minor *descending*

E harmonic minor

without key signatures:

with key signatures:

D harmonic minor

without key signatures:

with key signatures:

11 The Melodic Scales of A, E and D Minor

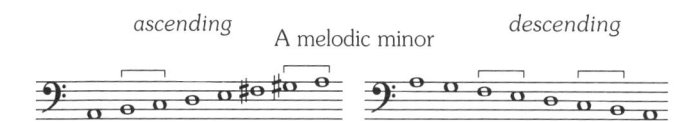

ascending A melodic minor *descending*

E melodic minor

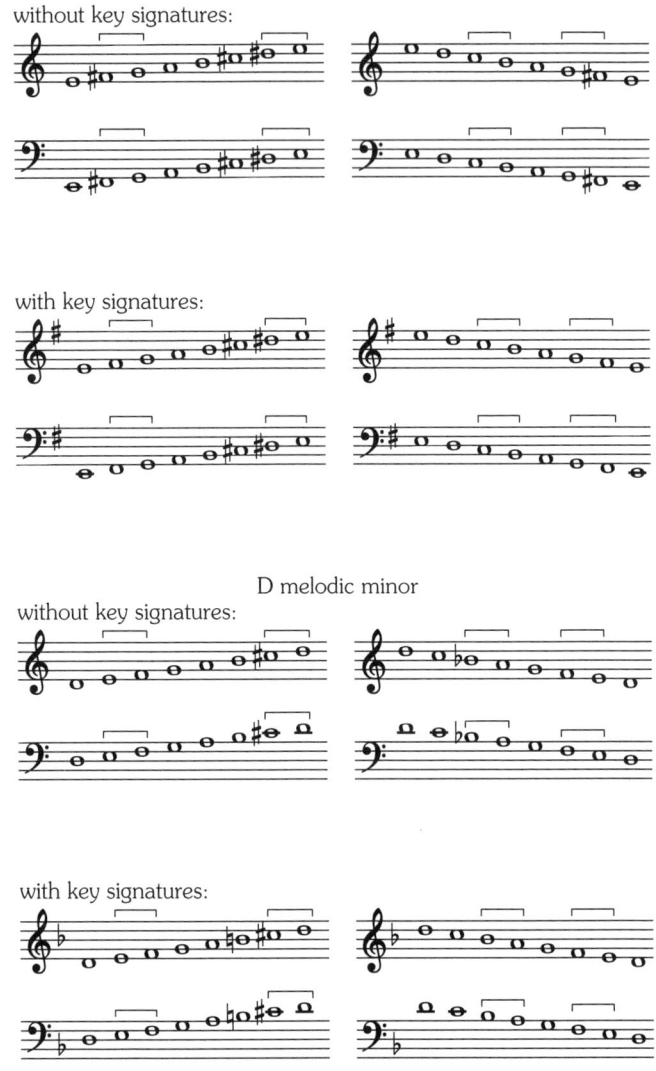

without key signatures:

with key signatures:

D melodic minor

without key signatures:

with key signatures:

12 Relative Major and Minor Keys

The words 'harmonic' and 'melodic' describe minor *scales*, not minor *keys*. This is because a piece of music in a minor key may use notes taken from both forms of the minor scale. Therefore a piece is simply 'in E minor' or 'in D minor' etc., not 'in E harmonic minor' or 'D melodic minor' etc.

You can see in the minor scales printed in Sections 10 and 11 above that:
- the key signatures of minor keys do not contain all the sharps or flats which may be needed;
- the key of A minor, like the key of C major, has no key signature;
- the key of E minor, like the key of G major, has a key signature of one sharp: F♯;
- the key of D minor, like the key of F major, has a key signature of one flat: B♭.

When a minor key has the same key signature as a major key it is the 'relative minor' of the major key. Similarly, a major key is the 'relative major' of the minor key with the same key signature. The same is true of the keys of A minor and C major, which have no key signatures. Therefore:

- the key of A minor is the relative minor of the key of C major, and
  the key of C major is the relative major of the key of A minor;

- the key of E minor is the relative minor of the key of G major, and
  the key of G major is the relative major of the key of E minor;

- the key of D minor is the relative minor of the key of F major, and
  the key of F major is the relative major of the key of D minor.

Although a major key and a minor key may have the same key signature, they are *different* keys. They have different keynotes (tonic notes) and different tonic triads. Compare the tonic notes (in brackets) and tonic triads of these keys:

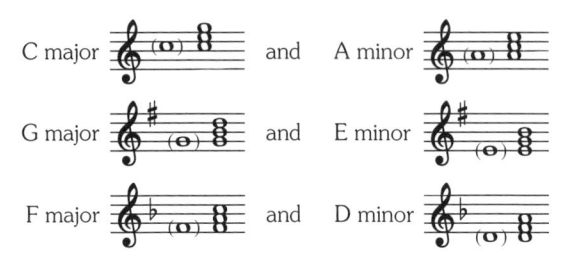

C major   and   A minor

G major   and   E minor

F major   and   D minor

You will see in later Grades that every major key has a relative minor key and, similarly, every minor key has a relative major key.

13 Intervals

The questions on intervals in Grade 2 will include questions using the new scales in this Grade — both major and minor. As in Grade 1, the lower note of the interval will always be the keynote of the scale, and you will have to know only the *number* of the interval. The number of an interval is the number of letter names which it contains, and this stays the same whether the scale is major or minor. For example, both of these are intervals of a 3rd, since they both include three letter names:

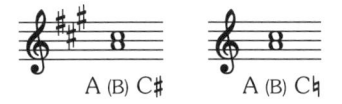

A (B) C♯   A (B) C♮

It makes no difference to the *number* of the interval that C is C♯ in the first example but C♮ in the second example.

Remember that if the two notes forming an interval are played together (as above) the interval is 'harmonic'. If they are played one after the other, they make a 'melodic' interval, and it does not matter which of the two is played first: both of the intervals marked ⌐——¬ here are a 5th:

14 Performance Directions (Terms and Signs)

Below is a list of Italian words and their meanings which, in addition to those in Grade 1, you should know in Grade 2. (It is the same as the list printed in *Music Theory in Practice*, Grade 2.)

a	at, to, by, for, in, in the style of
al, alla	to the, in the manner of (*alla marcia*: in the style of a march)
allargando	broadening (getting a little slower and probably a little louder)
andantino	slightly faster than *andante* (but may also mean slightly slower)
assai	very (*allegro assai*: very quick)
con, col	with
dolce	sweet, soft
e, ed	and
espressivo (or *espress.* or *espr.*)	expressive
fp (= *fortepiano*)	loud, then immediately soft
giocoso	playful, merry

grave	very slow, solemn
grazioso	graceful
larghetto	rather slow (but not as slow as *largo*)
largo	slow, stately
ma	but
maestoso	majestic
meno	less
molto	very, much
mosso, moto	movement (*meno mosso*: slower; *con moto*: with movement)
non	not
più	more
presto	fast (faster than *allegro*)
senza	without
sf, sfz (= *sforzando* or *sforzato*)	forced, accented
simile (or *sim.*)	in the same way
sostenuto	sustained
tenuto	held
troppo	too much (*non troppo*: not too much)
vivace, vivo	lively, quick

You should also know these signs:

The sign > over or under a note means that it is to be accented. ∧ (over) and ∨ (under) mean the same, or even stronger accents.

Dots inside a slur mean that the notes should be slightly separated (semi-staccato), but less so than notes with ordinary staccato dots.

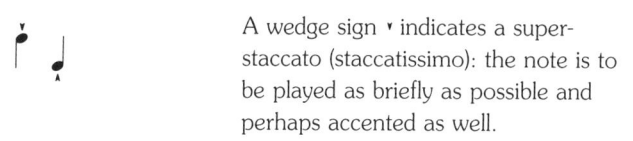

A wedge sign ▾ indicates a super-staccato (staccatissimo): the note is to be played as briefly as possible and perhaps accented as well.

The sign – means that the note is to be given a slight pressure (and generally slightly separated).

Grade 3

1 Simple and Compound Time

Music is in **simple time** when the beats divide into two equal notes. The time signatures used in Grades 1 and 2 were all examples of simple time signatures:

in $\frac{2}{4}$, $\frac{3}{4}$ and $\frac{4}{4}$ the ♩ beat divides into ♪ ♪ (♫)

in $\frac{2}{2}$, $\frac{3}{2}$ and $\frac{4}{2}$ the 𝅗𝅥 beat divides into ♩ ♩

in $\frac{3}{8}$ the ♪ beat divides into ♪ ♪ (♫)

Grade 3 introduces time signatures of a different kind: **compound time**. In compound time the beats divide into *three* equal notes, and the beats are written as *dotted* notes. The compound time signatures in Grade 3 all use a dotted crotchet (dotted quarter note) as the sign for a single beat. Here, for instance, there are two dotted crotchet beats in a bar:

| ♩. ♩. | ♫♪ ♫♪ |

The time signature for two dotted crotchet beats in a bar is $\frac{6}{8}$, meaning that there are six quavers in a bar. This can be confusing, because there are also six quavers in a bar of $\frac{3}{4}$; but in $\frac{3}{4}$ the six quavers would be the equivalent of *three crotchet* beats. Compare

$\frac{6}{8}$ ♫♪ ♫♪ | ♩. ♩. | with

$\frac{3}{4}$ ♫ ♫ ♫ | ♩ ♩ ♩ |

We saw in Grade 2 that it is possible to divide a simple time beat into three equal notes by writing the three notes as a triplet. So these two rhythms, for example, sound exactly the same, even though they are written differently:

$\frac{2}{4}$ 𝅘𝅥𝅮𝅘𝅥𝅮𝅘𝅥𝅮³ 𝅘𝅥𝅮𝅘𝅥𝅮𝅘𝅥𝅮³ | 𝅘𝅥 𝅘𝅥 |

$\frac{6}{8}$ 𝅘𝅥𝅮𝅘𝅥𝅮𝅘𝅥𝅮 𝅘𝅥𝅮𝅘𝅥𝅮𝅘𝅥𝅮 | 𝅘𝅥. 𝅘𝅥. |

Nevertheless, a triplet is an exception to the general rule that simple time beats divide into two, not three.

The compound time signatures in Grade 3 are $\frac{6}{8}$, $\frac{9}{8}$ and $\frac{12}{8}$.

$\frac{6}{8}$ has two (dotted crotchet) beats in a bar, so it is in compound duple time.

$\frac{9}{8}$ has three (dotted crotchet) beats in a bar, so it is in compound triple time.

$\frac{12}{8}$ has four (dotted crotchet) beats in a bar, so it is in compound quadruple time.

Here you can compare these compound time signatures with the simple duple, triple and quadruple time signatures which you studied in Grade 1:

Simple duple time

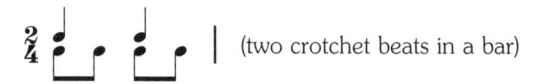

$\frac{2}{4}$ 𝅘𝅥 𝅘𝅥𝅮 𝅘𝅥 𝅘𝅥𝅮 | (two crotchet beats in a bar)

Compound duple time

$\frac{6}{8}$ 𝅘𝅥. 𝅘𝅥𝅮 𝅘𝅥𝅮 𝅘𝅥. 𝅘𝅥𝅮 𝅘𝅥𝅮 | (two dotted crotchet beats in a bar)

Simple triple time

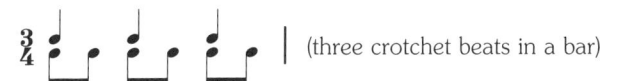

$\frac{3}{4}$ ♩♩ ♩♩ ♩♩ | (three crotchet beats in a bar)

Compound triple time

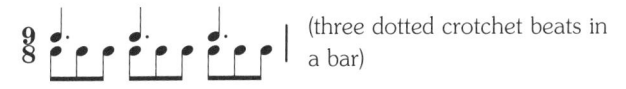

$\frac{9}{8}$ ♩.♩♩♩ ♩.♩♩♩ ♩.♩♩♩ | (three dotted crotchet beats in a bar)

Simple quadruple time

$\frac{4}{4}$ ♩♩ ♩♩ ♩♩ ♩♩ | (four crotchet beats in a bar)

Compound quadruple time

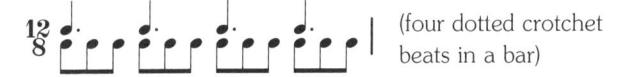

$\frac{12}{8}$ ♩.♩♩♩ ♩.♩♩♩ ♩.♩♩♩ ♩.♩♩♩ | (four dotted crotchet beats in a bar)

2 The Grouping of Notes in $\frac{6}{8}$, $\frac{9}{8}$ and $\frac{12}{8}$

Two full beats in compound time are written 𝅗𝅥. not ♩. ♩. .
Therefore 𝅗𝅥. should not be replaced by ♩. ♩. in any of these bars:

$\frac{6}{8}$ 𝅗𝅥. | $\frac{9}{8}$ 𝅗𝅥. ♩. | $\frac{9}{8}$ ♩. 𝅗𝅥. | $\frac{12}{8}$ 𝅗𝅥. 𝅗𝅥. | $\frac{12}{8}$ ♩.𝅗𝅥. ♩.|

In $^9_8$ and $^{12}_8$ a note lasting three full beats is written thus:

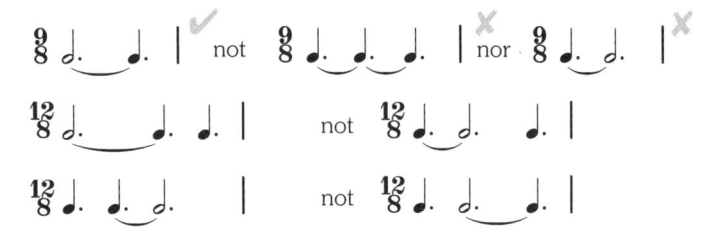

$^9_8$ 𝅗𝅭 — 𝅗𝅭 | not $^9_8$ 𝅗𝅭 — 𝅗𝅭 — 𝅗𝅭 | nor $^9_8$ 𝅗𝅭 — 𝅗𝅭 |

$^{12}_8$ 𝅗𝅭 —— 𝅗𝅭 𝅗𝅭 | not $^{12}_8$ 𝅗𝅭 — 𝅗𝅭 𝅗𝅭 |

$^{12}_8$ 𝅗𝅭 𝅗𝅭 — 𝅗𝅭 | not $^{12}_8$ 𝅗𝅭 𝅗𝅭 — 𝅗𝅭 |

In $^{12}_8$ a note lasting four full beats is written thus:

$^{12}_8$ 𝅝𝅭 | not $^{12}_8$ 𝅗𝅭 — 𝅗𝅭 |

Groups of notes adding up to complete beats are beamed together in *single* beats, thus:

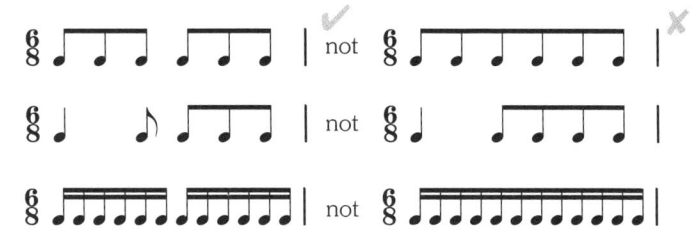

$^6_8$ ♩♩♩ ♩♩♩ | not $^6_8$ ♩♩♩♩♩♩ |

$^6_8$ ♩ ♪ ♩♩♩ | not $^6_8$ ♩ ♩♩♩♩ |

$^6_8$ ♫♫♫ ♫♫♫ | not $^6_8$ ♫♫♫♫♫♫ |

Ties *within* a beat should be avoided:

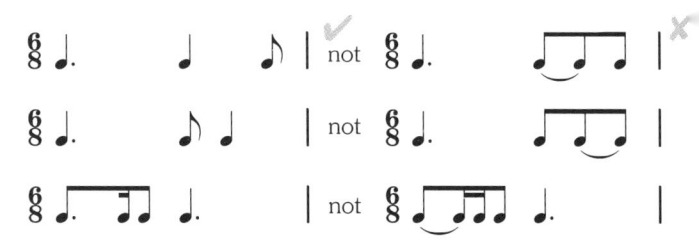

$^6_8$ 𝅗𝅭   ♩ ♪ | not $^6_8$ 𝅗𝅭 ♩—♩♩ |

$^6_8$ 𝅗𝅭   ♪ ♩ | not $^6_8$ 𝅗𝅭 ♪♩—♩ |

$^6_8$ ♩. ♫ ♩. | not $^6_8$ ♩♪—♫ ♩. |

but when a note is tied across a beat a tie *has* to be used:

The tie between notes makes it easier for a player to see at a glance where the beat comes. Notice the position of the beat marked ↑ in these further examples where ties are necessary:

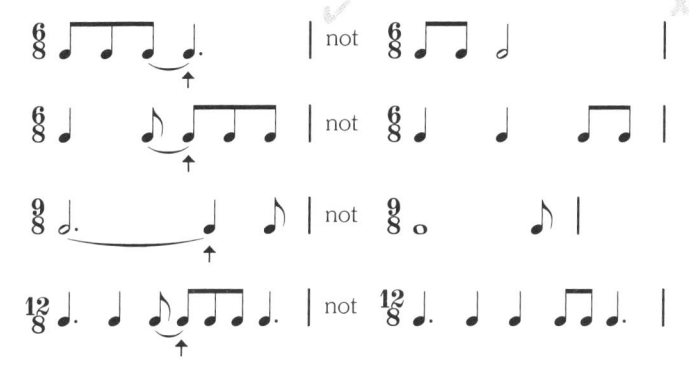

3 The Grouping of Rests in $\frac{6}{8}$, $\frac{9}{8}$ and $\frac{12}{8}$

In all these time signatures a completely silent bar is shown by a semibreve rest (without a dot):

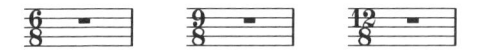

A silent *beat* may be shown in two ways: either by a dotted crotchet rest (𝄽·) or by a crotchet rest followed by a quaver rest (𝄽 𝄾). Both of these examples are correct and mean the same thing:

You are free to use whichever of the two ways you prefer, but 𝄽 is generally clearer (and is used in the examples given later in this section). Notice that the following arrangements of rests are WRONG:

$$\frac{6}{8} \; ♩. \; 𝄾 \; 𝄽 \; | \; 𝄾 \; 𝄽 \; ♩. \; | \quad \text{and} \quad \frac{6}{8} \; ♩. \; 𝄾 \; 𝄾 \; 𝄾 \; | \; 𝄾 \; 𝄾 \; 𝄾 \; ♩. \; |$$

In compound time, as in simple time, every new beat in a silence needs a new rest, except in the first or second half of a four-beat bar. Compare these examples in simple time with the compound time versions underneath:

Simple triple time

$$\frac{3}{4} \; 𝄽 \; 𝄽 \; ♩ \; | \; ♩ \; 𝄽 \; 𝄽 \; | \quad \text{not} \quad \frac{3}{4} \; 𝄼 \; ♩ \; | \; ♩ \; 𝄼 \; |$$

Compound triple time

$$\frac{9}{8} \; 𝄽 \; 𝄽 \; ♩. \; | \; ♩. \; 𝄽 \; 𝄽 \; | \quad \text{not} \quad \frac{9}{8} \; 𝄼. \; ♩. \; | \; ♩. \; 𝄼. \; |$$

Simple quadruple time

$$\frac{4}{4} \; 𝄼 \; 𝄽 \; ♩ \; | \; ♩ \; 𝄽 \; 𝄼 \; |$$

Compound quadruple time

$$\frac{12}{8} \; 𝄼. \; 𝄽. \; ♩. \; | \; ♩. \; 𝄽. \; 𝄼. \; |$$

Simple quadruple time

$$\frac{4}{4} \; 𝄼 \; ♩ \; | \; ♩ \; 𝄼 \; | \quad \text{not} \quad \frac{4}{4} \; 𝄽 \; 𝄽 \; ♩ \; | \; ♩ \; 𝄽 \; 𝄽 \; |$$

Compound quadruple time

$$\frac{12}{8} \; 𝄼. \; ♩. \; | \; ♩. \; 𝄼. \; | \quad \text{not} \quad \frac{12}{8} \; 𝄽 \; 𝄽 \; ♩. \; | \; ♩. \; 𝄽 \; 𝄽 \; |$$

Simple quadruple time

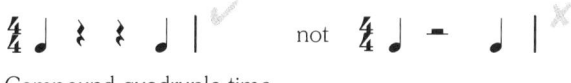

$\frac{4}{4}$ ♩ 𝄽 𝄽 ♩ | ✓   not $\frac{4}{4}$ ♩ — ♩ | ✗

Compound quadruple time

$\frac{12}{8}$ ♩. 𝄽· 𝄽· ♩. | ✓   not $\frac{12}{8}$ ♩. —· ♩. | ✗

Notice that in compound time, as in simple time, two-beat *rests* in the middle of a four-beat bar are treated differently from two-beat *notes*:

$\frac{12}{8}$ ♩. 𝄽· 𝄽· ♩. | is correct

but $\frac{12}{8}$ ♩. ♩. ♩. ♩. | would be incorrect

$\frac{12}{8}$ ♩. ♩.   ♩. | is correct

but $\frac{12}{8}$ ♩. —·   ♩. | would be incorrect

When you are dealing with silences of *less* than a full beat, you have to remember that a beat in compound time has three main divisions (♩. = ♪♪♪), not two as in simple time (♩ = ♪♪). Quaver and crotchet rests *within* a ♩. beat are arranged as follows (the ⌐¬ marks have been added as a reminder that each group is in the time of a ♩. beat):

𝄾 ♩

♩ 𝄾

𝄽 ♪   (This is now standard, although 𝄾 𝄾 ♪ was often written in earlier days.)

♪ 𝄾 𝄾   not   ♪ 𝄽

Again, compare these examples in simple time with the compound time examples underneath:

Simple duple time $\quad \mathbf{^2_4}$ ♩ | ♩ 𝄽 |

Compound duple time $\mathbf{^6_8}$ 𝄽· ♩ | ♩ 𝄽· |

Simple triple time $\quad \mathbf{^3_4}$ 𝄽 𝄽 ♪ | ♪ 𝄽 𝄽 |

Compound triple time $\mathbf{^9_8}$ 𝄽· 𝄽· ♪ | ♪ 𝄽· |

Simple quadruple time $\quad \mathbf{^4_4}$ — 𝄽 ♪ | ♪ 𝄽 — |

Compound quadruple time $\mathbf{^{12}_{8}}$ — 𝄽· ♪ | ♪ 𝄽· — |

Each ♪ in the examples above can be divided into 𝄽 ♬ or ♬ 𝄽 as usual (see Grade 2, p. 36). For example:

Simple duple time $\quad \mathbf{^2_4}$ 𝄽 ♬ | ♬ 𝄽 |

Compound duple time $\mathbf{^6_8}$ 𝄽· ♬ | ♬ 𝄽· |

Below are some examples of semiquaver rests in complete bars. Notice that beaming helps to make the rhythmic grouping clear:

[music notation examples in 6/8, 6/8, 6/8 or 6/8, and 9/8]

4 Demisemiquaver Notes and Rests

Grade 3 introduces a note with half the time value of a semiquaver: the **demisemiquaver** or '32nd note'. The note has three flags ♪, and the rest has three hooks ✸. When demisemiquavers are beamed together they have three beams ♫. So:

a ♪ has the same time value as ♫

a ♪ has the same time value as ♫

a ♩ has the same time value as ♫

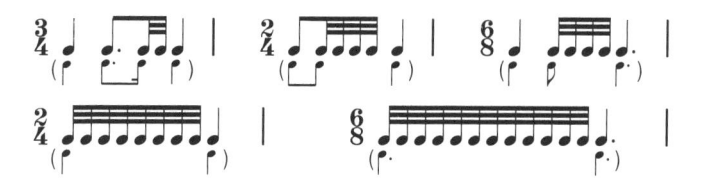

Demisemiquavers are beamed together when they could be replaced by a ♪, a ♪, a ♩, or by a ♩. in compound time. Compare each of these examples with the rhythm in brackets underneath:

However, eight or twelve ♪s may also be beamed in groups of four:

and beaming them in this way often makes the music easier to read.

More complicated patterns of ♫s are certainly easier to read if the notes are beamed in subdivisions of a ♩ or (in compound time) a ♩. beat. For instance, these examples are best written:

[music example in 2/4] not [music example in 2/4]

[music example in 6/8] not [music example in 6/8]

Demisemiquaver rests are arranged in the same way as quaver and semiquaver rests. These two examples follow the same pattern as the examples on page 60:

Simple duple time [music example in 2/4]

Compound duple time

[music example in 6/8]

5 Upbeat Starts

A piece of music may begin with a note or a group of notes *before* the first bar line:

Schumann: 'The Merry Peasant', from *Album for the Young*

[music example] etc.

Traditional: 'The First Nowell'

[music example] etc.

This kind of opening is called an 'upbeat' start, because a conductor's baton or hand moves upwards before the downbeat at the beginning of a bar. It is also known as an 'anacrusis'. Many examples of upbeat starts are given in Grade 3 of *Music Theory in Practice*, particularly in Section I, which explains how to use an upbeat start in the four-bar rhythm which you may be asked to compose.

Upbeat starts often set a pattern for an entire piece, as in this simple example:

Traditional: 'The British Grenadiers'

Here the opening four-bar rhythm (marked A1⎦) is immediately repeated (A2). Then there is a different four-bar rhythm (B), although it too starts with an upbeat. Finally A1 is repeated again (A3).[1]

Notice that A1 does not finish at the *end* of bar 4: it finishes with the quaver rest. Similarly, A2 finishes with the quaver rest in bar 8, and A3 with the quaver rest in the last bar. As a result, the last bar is not a full bar (a full bar would have a crotchet rest). The upbeat quaver at the beginning makes up for the 'missing' quaver at the end.

This explains something which you will often find in pieces which start with an upbeat: the value of the note or notes before the bar line at the beginning is deducted from the last bar. In

---

[1] A3 has become better known in a varied form.

other words, the time values of the upbeat opening plus the time values of the incomplete bar at the end 'add up' to a full bar. Therefore:

a piece beginning $\frac{2}{4}$ ♩ | could end | ♩ ||

a piece beginning $\frac{3}{4}$ ♩ | could end | ♩ ||

a piece beginning $\frac{6}{8}$ ♪ | could end | ♩. ♩ ||

a piece beginning $\frac{4}{4}$ ♩ | could end | ♩. ||

Of course, an incomplete bar at the end can include more than one note, or a mixture of notes and rests, provided their total value is correct. But they must be grouped in the usual way up to the point where the bar stops short. What this means in practice is that they must be grouped *as though* they were followed by the upbeat notes at the beginning. For instance:

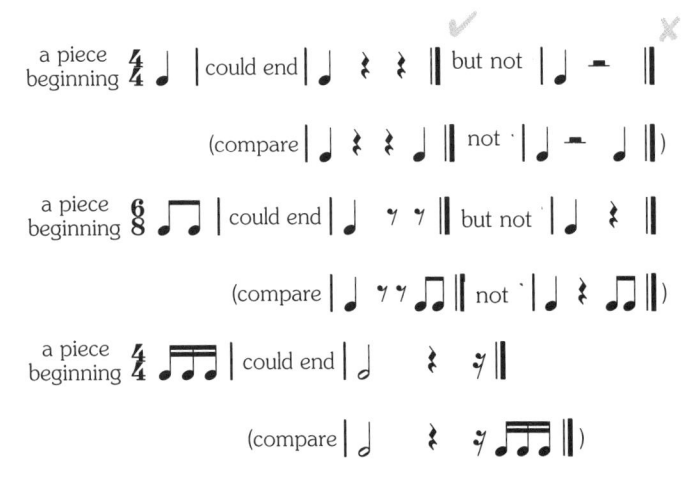

a piece beginning $\frac{4}{4}$ ♩ | could end | ♩ 𝄾 𝄾 || but not | ♩ 𝄼 ||

(compare | ♩ 𝄾 𝄾 ♩ || not ·| ♩ 𝄼 ♩ ||)

a piece beginning $\frac{6}{8}$ ♫ | could end | ♩ 𝄾 𝄾 || but not | ♩ 𝄾 ||

(compare | ♩ 𝄾 𝄾 ♫ || not ·| ♩ 𝄾 ♫ ||)

a piece beginning $\frac{4}{4}$ ♬ | could end | ♩ 𝄾 𝄾 ||

(compare | ♩ 𝄾 𝄾 ♬ ||)

If a section of music beginning with an upbeat is repeated, the repeat can be shown by the usual repeat sign (see Grade 1, p. 28). 'The British Grenadiers', quoted above, is an example. A2 is exactly the same as A1, so it does not *have* to be written out again: it could be shown by a repeat mark instead. However, the repeat mark must be in exactly the right place, which is after the quaver rest in bar 4. Note that it is followed by a double bar line, and that the passage marked ⌐—x—⌐ 'adds up' to a full bar:

The sections marked A1, A2 etc. in 'The British Grenadiers' are examples of musical 'phrases'. For further examples and more information about phrases see *Music Theory in Practice*, Grade 3 and *The AB Guide to Music Theory*, Part I, 9/1.

6 Ledger Lines and Octave Signs

In this Grade you may be asked to name or write notes with more than two ledger lines. These, of course, simply continue from where we left off in Grade 2 (p. 38):

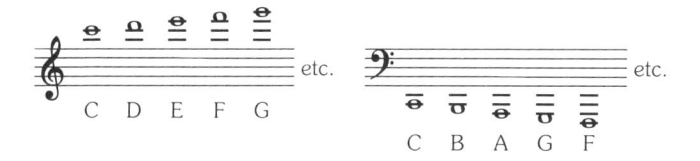

C D E F G   C B A G F

However, another way of writing very high or very low notes is by using octave signs above or below the notes to show that they are to be played an octave higher or lower (see Grade 1, p. 28). For example,

can be written as

and

can be written as

7 Octave Transposition

These two melodies are the same, except that the notes in (b) are all an octave lower than the notes in (a):

The second melody is a **transposition** of the first. Music is 'transposed' when it is rewritten so that it will sound higher or lower (or when it is simply *performed* higher or lower, without being written out again).

At (b) the melody of (a) was transposed 'down an octave'. The transposed version could of course be written in the bass clef, thus:

(c)

but that would not change the transposition. The melody of (a) has still been transposed down an octave in (c).

In the examination you may be asked to write a melody an octave higher or lower, and using a bass clef instead of a treble clef (or a treble clef instead of a bass clef). For example, if you had been asked to write melody (a) 'an octave lower in the bass clef' the correct answer would have been (c). Similarly, if you were asked to write this melody:

'an octave higher in the treble clef' the answer would be:

8 The Major Scales of E and A Flat

In Grade 3 you will be expected to know the scales and key signatures using up to four sharps or four flats. The new major scales are E major (four sharps) and A♭ major (four flats). In E major the new sharp is D♯, and in A♭ major the new flat is D♭. Here are their key signatures and tonic chords:

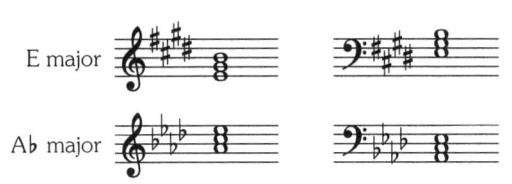

E major

A♭ major

These are the scales:

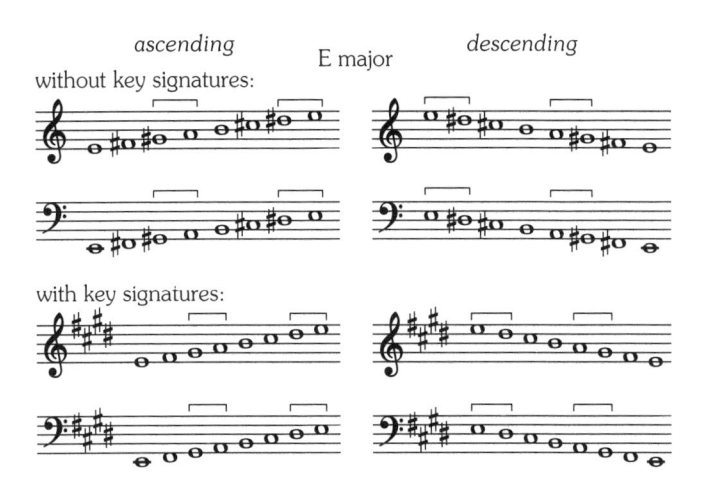

ascending E major *descending*

without key signatures:

with key signatures:

A♭ major

without key signatures:

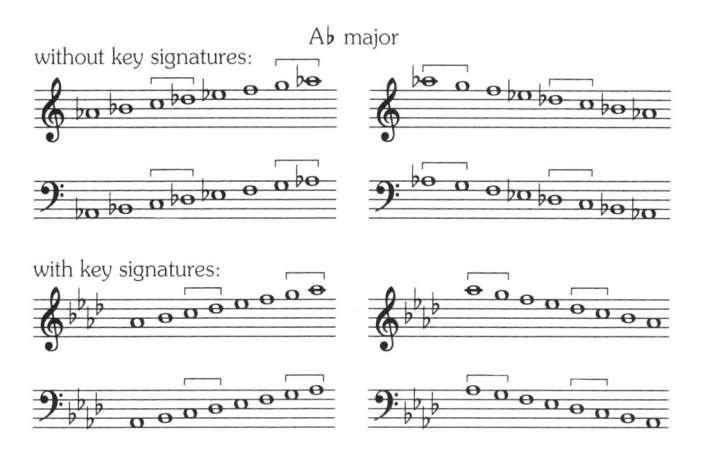

with key signatures:

9 The Minor Scales of B, F Sharp and C Sharp

The new minor scales with sharp key signatures are:
- B minor, with two sharps (F♯ and C♯)
- F♯ minor, with three sharps (F♯, C♯ and G♯)
- C♯ minor, with four sharps (F♯, C♯, G♯ and D♯)

You will be expected to know both the harmonic and the melodic forms of these scales (and of the minor scales set in Grade 2).

Notice that B minor has the same key signature as D major. Therefore:
- B minor is the relative minor of D major. Similarly,
- F♯ minor is the relative minor of A major, and
- C♯ minor is the relative minor of E major.

But the minor keys of course have different tonic chords from their relative majors. Here are the key signatures and tonic chords together:

B minor

F# minor

C# minor

Below is a representative selection of the scales of all the above keys:

ascending B harmonic minor *descending*

without key signatures:

with key signatures:

B melodic minor

without key signatures:

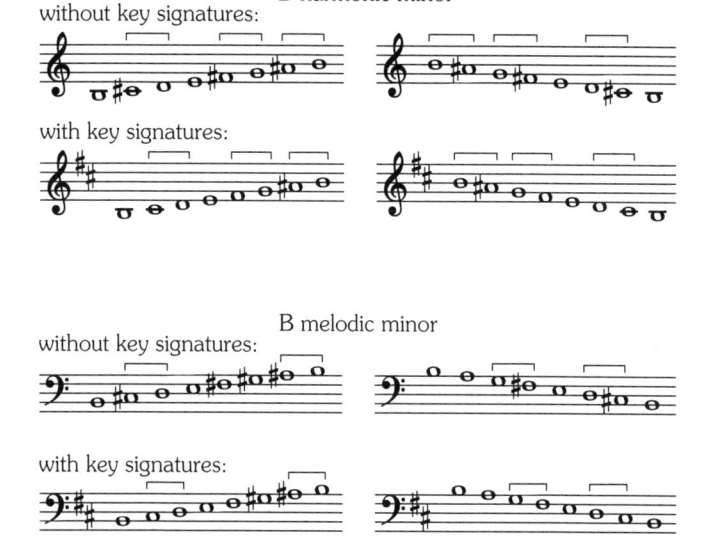

with key signatures:

F♯ harmonic minor

without key signatures:

F♯ melodic minor

with key signatures:

C♯ harmonic minor

with key signatures:

C♯ melodic minor

without key signatures:

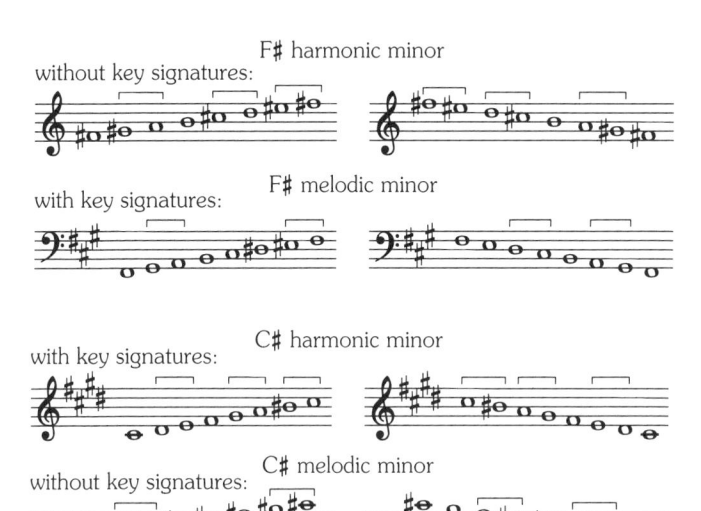

10 The Minor Scales of G, C and F

The new minor scales with flat key signatures are:
- G minor, with two flats   (B♭ and E♭)
- C minor, with three flats (B♭, E♭ and A♭)
- F minor, with four flats   (B♭, E♭, A♭ and D♭)

Therefore:
- G minor is the relative minor of B♭ major,
- C minor is the relative minor of E♭ major, and
- F minor is the relative minor of A♭ major.

These are the key signatures and tonic chords of the minor keys with flats:

G minor

C minor

F minor

Below are examples of the scales in all these keys:

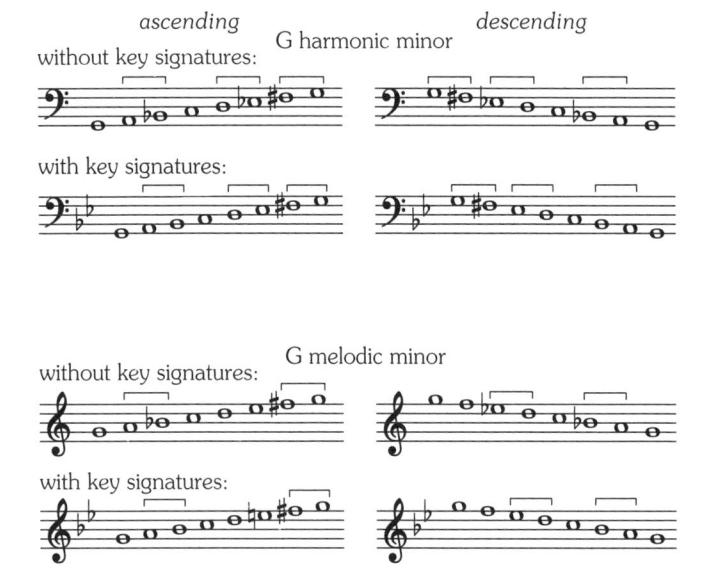

G harmonic minor

ascending — *descending*

without key signatures:

with key signatures:

G melodic minor

without key signatures:

with key signatures:

without key signatures: C harmonic minor

with key signatures: C melodic minor

with key signatures: F harmonic minor

without key signatures: F melodic minor

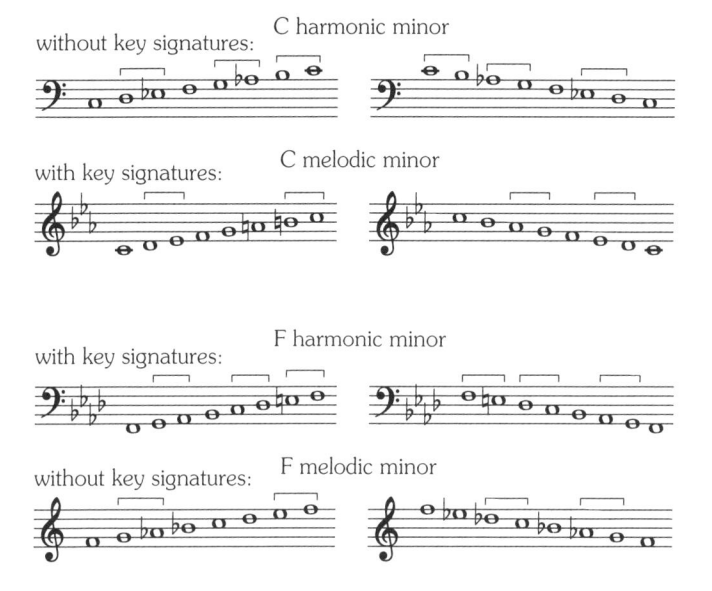

11 Intervals

In earlier Grades you were asked to name only the 'number' of an interval. But the number of an interval is not a full description of it. For example, both of these are a 3rd:

and

yet they are not exactly the same. Grade 3 makes a start at naming intervals *exactly*, although both notes of the interval will belong to one of the scales you have studied, and the lower note will still be the keynote (tonic).

In every major and minor scale, the intervals produced by the

4th and 5th degrees above the tonic, and by the octave, are all described as 'perfect':

perfect 4th, perfect 5th, perfect 8ve and *perfect 4th, perfect 5th, perfect 8ve*

Note that these intervals are always the same both in major and in minor keys. The 2nd degree also remains the same, and the interval it produces is always a 'major' 2nd (even in minor keys):

major 2nd and *major 2nd*

However, the other intervals (3rd, 6th and 7th) are not always the same. The 3rd is a 'major' 3rd in a major key:

major 3rd

but a 'minor' 3rd in a minor key:

minor 3rd

In a major key the 6th and 7th degrees make major intervals with the tonic:

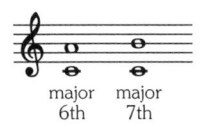

major 6th, major 7th

But in a minor key there are two different forms of the 6th degree and two different forms of the 7th degree (compare the ascending and descending forms of a melodic minor scale). When they are the same as in a major key, the intervals they produce are still major:

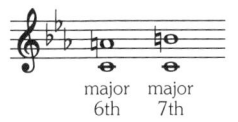

[musical notation: major 6th, major 7th]

But when the lower forms of the 6th and 7th degrees are used, the intervals become minor:

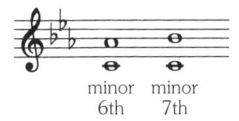

[musical notation: minor 6th, minor 7th]

Putting all these together, we get the following intervals above C, the keynote of the scales of C major and C minor:

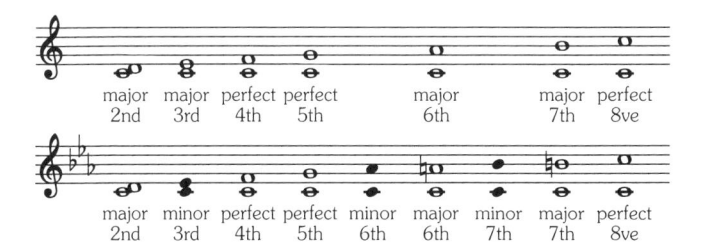

[musical notation: major 2nd, major 3rd, perfect 4th, perfect 5th, major 6th, major 7th, perfect 8ve]

[musical notation: major 2nd, minor 3rd, perfect 4th, perfect 5th, minor 6th, major 6th, minor 7th, major 7th, perfect 8ve]

This pattern of intervals is unchanged in all other keys, even though they may require different accidentals, for example, in E major and E minor:

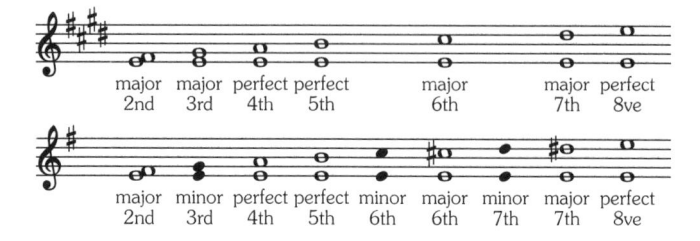

(E major scale intervals)
major 2nd, major 3rd, perfect 4th, perfect 5th, major 6th, major 7th, perfect 8ve

(E minor scale intervals)
major 2nd, minor 3rd, perfect 4th, perfect 5th, minor 6th, major 6th, minor 7th, major 7th, perfect 8ve

The words major, minor and perfect (and others which we shall meet in Grade 4) describe the 'quality' of an interval. Thus the 'number' of this interval:

is a 2nd, and its quality is major.

12 Performance Directions

Below is a list of Italian words and their meanings (in addition to those in earlier Grades) which you should know in Grade 3. (It is the same as the list printed in *Music Theory in Practice*, Grade 3.)

adagietto	rather slow (but faster than *adagio*)
ad libitum, ad lib.	at choice, meaning that a passage may be played freely
agitato	agitated
alla breve	with a minim beat, equivalent to ¢ ($\frac{2}{2}$), implying a faster tempo than the note values might otherwise suggest

amore	love (*amoroso*: loving)
anima	soul, spirit (*con anima* can mean 'with feeling' or 'spirited')
animato	animated, lively (*animando*: becoming more lively)
ben	well
brio	vigour (*con brio*: with vigour, lively)
comodo	convenient (*tempo comodo*: at a comfortable speed)
deciso	with determination
delicato	delicate
energico	energetic
forza	force
largamente	broadly
leggiero	light, nimble
marcato, *marc.*	emphatic, accented
marziale	in a military style
mesto	sad
pesante	heavy
prima, *primo*	first
risoluto	bold, strong
ritmico	rhythmically
rubato, *tempo rubato*	with some freedom of time
scherzando, *scherzoso*	playful, joking
seconda, *secondo*	second
semplice	simple, plain
sempre	always
stringendo	gradually getting faster
subito	suddenly
tanto	so much
tranquillo	calm
triste, *tristamente*	sad, sorrowful
volta	time (*prima volta*: first time; *seconda volta*: second time)

Grade 4

1 Breves

A **breve** or 'double whole note' is a note with the time value of two semibreves (= four minims or eight crotchets etc.). Therefore it fills an entire bar of $\frac{4}{2}$. It may be written in two ways: either as |o| or as ⊐ . A silent bar in $\frac{4}{2}$ is shown by a breve rest:

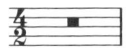

Notice that it completely fills the space between the third and fourth stave lines. $\frac{4}{2}$ is the only time signature in which a silent bar is not shown by a semibreve rest.

2 Double Dots

We saw in Grade 1 that a dot after a note makes it longer by half its value:

$$\text{d.} = \text{d}\_\text{d} \qquad \text{J.} = \text{J}\_\text{♪} \qquad \text{♪.} = \text{♪}\_\text{♬}$$

A second dot after a note makes it even longer, by adding half the value which was added by the first dot:

$$\text{d..} = \text{d}\_\text{d}\_\text{♪} \qquad \text{J..} = \text{J}\_\text{♪}\_\text{♬} \qquad \text{♪..} = \text{♪}\_\text{♬}\_\text{♬}$$

Examples:

Similarly, a second dot after a dotted rest lengthens it by half the value which was added by the first dot. Strictly speaking, of course, a second dot breaks the convention that each subdivision of a beat should start with a new rest (see Grade 2, pp. 35–6, and Grade 3, p. 60). For instance, it would be standard practice to write

$\frac{4}{4}$ 𝄽 ♩ ♩ ♪♩ |

rather than

$\frac{4}{4}$ 𝄽·· ♪♩ |

Nevertheless, you may see double-dotted rests used in situations such as this last example, which is certainly clear.

3 Regular Time Signatures

Regular time signatures are those which indicate duple, triple or quadruple time — either simple or compound in each case. The regular time signatures which we have used in earlier grades are:

in simple time

$\frac{3}{8}$ (three quaver beats in a bar)

$\frac{2}{4}$ $\frac{3}{4}$ $\frac{4}{4}$ (two, three or four crotchet beats in a bar)

$\frac{2}{2}$ $\frac{3}{2}$ $\frac{4}{2}$ (two, three or four minim beats in a bar)

in compound time

$\frac{6}{8}$ $\frac{9}{8}$ $\frac{12}{8}$ (two, three or four dotted crotchet beats in a bar)

Grade 4 examinations may include questions on *all* regular time signatures. In practice, some of these are rare (e.g. $\frac{2}{8}$ — two quaver beats in a bar), or almost never used (e.g. $\frac{12}{2}$ — four dotted minim beats in a bar). However, all of these are common:

in simple time

$\frac{4}{8}$ (four quaver beats in a bar)

in compound time

$\frac{6}{4}$ $\frac{9}{4}$ (two or three dotted minim beats in a bar)

$\frac{6}{16}$ $\frac{9}{16}$ $\frac{12}{16}$ (two, three or four dotted quaver beats in a bar)

In $\frac{4}{8}$ the notes and rests are grouped just as they would be in $\frac{2}{4}$, e.g.:

The difference between the two is that $\frac{2}{4}$ indicates two (crotchet) beats in a bar, while $\frac{4}{8}$ indicates four (quaver) beats in a bar.

The grouping of notes and rests in the new compound time signatures is the same as in $\frac{6}{8}$, $\frac{9}{8}$ and $\frac{12}{8}$ (see Grade 3, Sections 2 and 3) except that:

in $\frac{6}{4}$ and $\frac{9}{4}$ the time values are doubled, and

in $\frac{6}{16}$, $\frac{9}{16}$ and $\frac{12}{16}$ the time values are halved. You can see this by comparing the following examples:

4 Duplets

In compound time (where the beats are dotted notes) a beat may be divided into two equal notes instead of the usual three. The two notes are called a **duplet**. A duplet, therefore, is a group of two equal notes which are performed in the time normally taken by three of them. It is shown by a figure 2 above or below the notes:

A different way of writing the same thing is to add a dot after each of the two notes:

By using duplets in compound time or triplets in simple time, it is possible to write a rhythm in *either* a compound time signature *or* a simple time signature. For instance, all the examples below sound exactly the same — provided that the speed of the beat (♩ ♩. ♩ or ♩.) remains the same in all the examples.

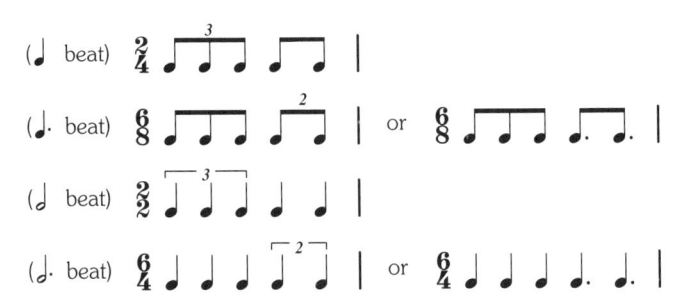

5 Double Sharps and Flats; Enharmonic Equivalents

This sign ✗ is called a **double sharp**. It raises a note by *two* semitones, for example:

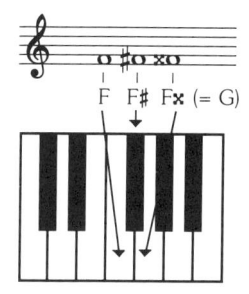

F F♯ F✗ (= G)

The sign which lowers a note by two semitones is a **double flat**. This is simply two flats together, ♭♭, for example:

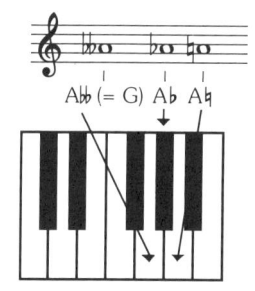

A♭♭ (= G) A♭ A♮

You can see from these examples that the note 'G' on the keyboard can also be called and written as F✗ or A♭♭. In fact, except for A♭/G♯, every note on the keyboard can have three names. For instance:

C	=	B♯	=	D♭♭
C♯	=	B✗	=	D♭
D	=	C✗	=	E♭♭
E♭	=	D♯	=	F♭♭
E	=	D✗	=	F♭ ...and so on.

Notes which sound the same but have different names are sometimes said to be 'spelt' differently. They are also described as **enharmonic equivalents**: B♯ is an enharmonic equivalent of C; so is D♭♭; and all three notes are enharmonic equivalents of each other.

6 The Scales of B Major and G Sharp Minor

The new scales in this Grade are those with five sharps or five flats, namely:
- B major and its relative minor, G♯ minor;
- D♭ major and its relative minor, B♭ minor.

The key signatures of the two 'sharp' keys (B major and G♯ minor) are:

ascending   B major   *descending*

Scales in each of these keys are given below. You will see that a double sharp (F𝄪) is required in G♯ minor scales. The F𝄪 cannot be replaced by G♮, its enharmonic equivalent, because there would then be no F of any kind in the scale.

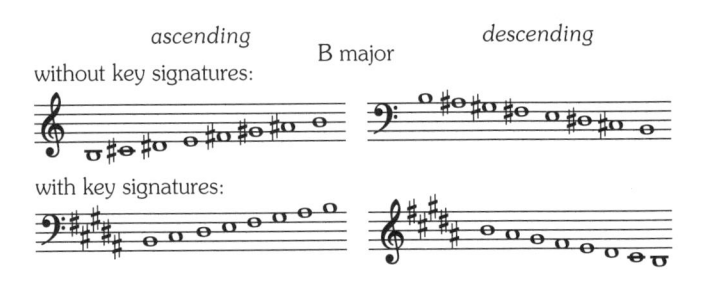

without key signatures:

with key signatures:

G♯ harmonic minor

without key signatures:

with key signatures:

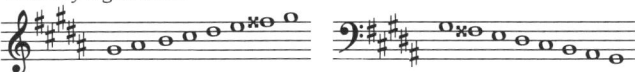

G♯ melodic minor

without key signatures:

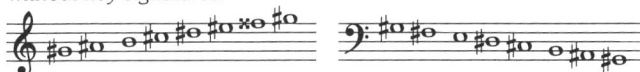

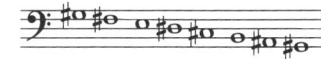

with key signatures:

7 The Scales of D Flat Major and B Flat Minor

The key signatures of the new 'flat' keys (D♭ major and B♭ minor) are:

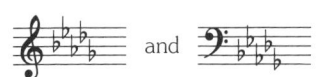

and

Here are examples of scales in these keys:

ascending   *descending*

D♭ major

without key signatures:

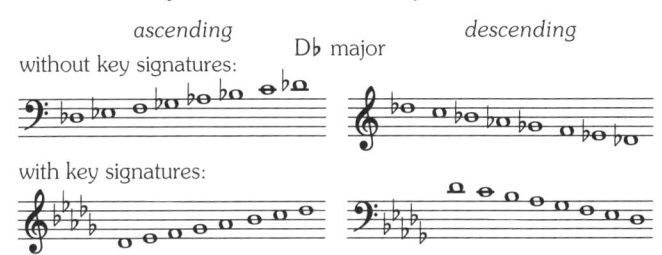

with key signatures:

B♭ harmonic minor

without key signatures:

with key signatures:

B♭ melodic minor

without key signatures:

with key signatures:

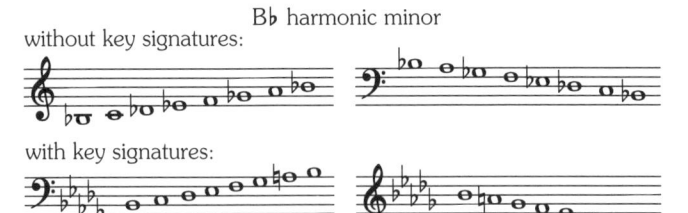

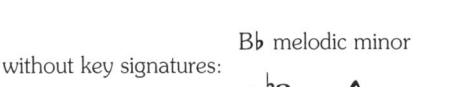

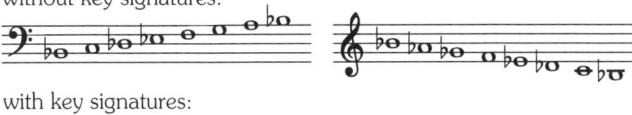

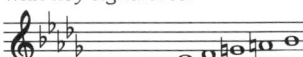

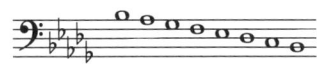

8 The Technical Names of Notes in Diatonic Scales

All major and minor scales are described as 'diatonic' scales. The various degrees of a diatonic scale (1st, 2nd, 3rd etc.) are known by names as well as by numbers. We have already used one of these names — the **tonic**, which is the technical name of the first degree of the scale. Here is a complete list:

1st degree:	tonic
2nd degree:	supertonic
3rd degree:	mediant
4th degree:	subdominant
5th degree:	dominant
6th degree:	submediant
7th degree:	leading note
8th degree:	(upper) tonic

The tonic is of course the 'keynote' — the basic pitch of a piece, the bass note on which the music ends. But the 5th degree of the scale, the **dominant**, can be said to 'dominate' the music since it has a special relationship with the tonic which gives it a particular importance in harmony. Another influential note is the 7th degree, the **leading note**, so called because when it appears in a melody it is often followed by the note above it (the tonic). In other words, the leading note 'leads' up to the tonic. Notice that the leading note is always the *major* 7th of the scale: it is always a *semitone* below the keynote, not only in major keys but also in minor keys. (When a minor 7th is used, as in the descending form of the melodic minor scale —

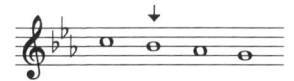

— it can be described as the 'lowered leading note' or 'flattened leading note'.)

The 2nd degree of the scale is called the **supertonic** because it is the note above ('super' in Latin) the tonic. The 3rd degree is the **mediant** (from a Latin word meaning 'in the middle') because it is the middle note between the tonic and the dominant. For example, in C major:

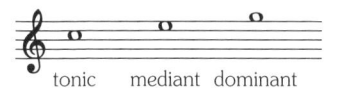

tonic   mediant dominant

The 4th degree did not become known as the **subdominant** because it is the note below ('sub') the dominant — although it is! — but for a more complicated reason. The subdominant is the same distance below the tonic as the dominant is above it:

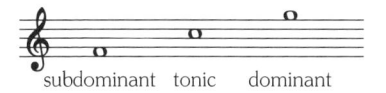

subdominant tonic   dominant

Similarly, the 6th degree, the **submediant**, is the same distance below the tonic as the mediant is above it:

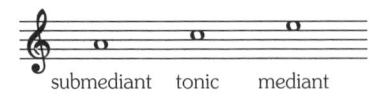

submediant   tonic   mediant

9 Intervals

The lower note of the intervals used in earlier Grades was always the tonic: the keynote of the scale. In Grade 4 you will be expected to know the interval between *any* two notes, provided that they both belong to one of the scales you have studied, and are not more than an octave apart.

At the end of the section on intervals in Grade 3, there were examples of all the intervals produced by the notes of the major and minor scales above the tonic (see pp. 75–6). What you need to know now is that *the name of an interval does not change if the same two notes are written with a different key signature*. For instance, all of these are perfect 5ths:

and all of these are minor 6ths:

Likewise, all these intervals are major 3rds:

(because G♯ is the 3rd degree of the major scale of E) even though none of them has a key signature of E major. Consequently there should be no difficulty about naming an interval if its lower note is the keynote of a major or minor scale which includes the upper note. The following examples name and explain the intervals marked ⌐ ¬.

(Key: F major)

a major 3rd, because E is the 3rd degree of the scale of C major;

(Key: C minor)

a minor 3rd, because D is the 3rd degree of the scale of B minor;

(Key: C major)

a perfect 5th, because A is the 5th degree of the scale of D major;

(Key: G major)

a minor 7th, because C is the 7th degree of the scale of D minor (melodic form, descending).

Naming an interval is more complicated when its lower note is *not* the keynote of a scale containing the upper note. For example, neither the scale of E♭ major nor the scale of E♭ minor includes the A♮ in this interval:

The interval must be a 4th (because it includes four letter names), but it is not a *perfect* 4th. It is a semitone *larger* than a perfect 4th on E♭:

and a semitone *larger* than a perfect 4th below A♮:

What, then, are we to call:

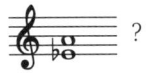

?

In Grade 3 we needed only three words to describe the quality of intervals: major, minor and perfect. Now we need two more: intervals may also be **diminished** or **augmented**. The ways in which intervals change their names when they are made a semitone smaller or larger (but keep the same letter names) can be summed up as follows:
- If the top note of an interval is lowered a semitone or the bottom note is raised a semitone —
    major intervals become minor,
    minor and perfect intervals become diminished.

- If the bottom note of an interval is lowered a semitone or the top note is raised a semitone —
    minor intervals become major,
    major and perfect intervals become augmented.

It may help you to remember these name changes if you think of them like this:

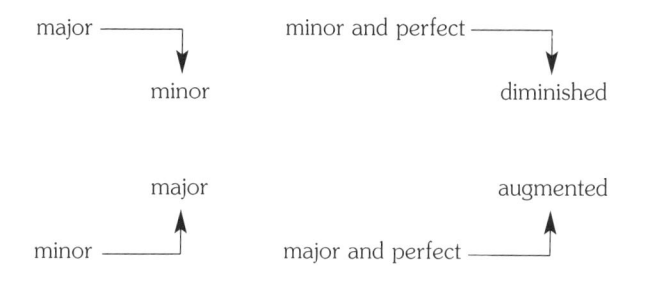

major ─────┐   minor and perfect ─────┐
           ▼   ▼
        minor   diminished

        major   augmented
          ▲   ▲
minor ────┘   major and perfect ─────────────────┘

We can now see that

is an *augmented* 4th, because it is a semitone larger than a perfect 4th. It is the interval between the 4th and 7th degrees of the scale of B♭ major:

or B♭ (harmonic) minor:

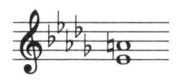

Here are two more examples:

(Key: E♭ major)

The interval

is a 2nd. D–E♮ would be a major 2nd (because E is the 2nd degree of the scale of D major); but D–E♭ is a semitone smaller so the interval is a *minor* 2nd.

(Key: B minor)

The interval

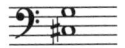

is a 5th. C♮–G would be a perfect 5th (because G is the 5th degree of the scale of C major); but C♯–G is a semitone smaller so the interval is a *diminished* 5th.

10 Triads on the Tonic, Subdominant and Dominant

A triad may be built on any note of a scale, not just the tonic. Grade 4 includes triads on the subdominant and dominant of the scales you have studied, as well as on the tonic. For example, in C major:

[Musical notation: treble clef, C major key signature, three triads labeled:]
tonic   subdominant   dominant

In minor keys the notes of triads are those of the *harmonic* form of the scale. Here are the same three triads in C minor:

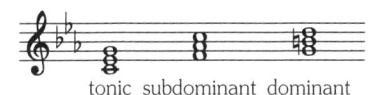

[Musical notation: treble clef, C minor key signature with three flats, three triads labeled:]
tonic   subdominant   dominant

The note on which a triad is built is called the **root** of the triad, so:
- the root of a tonic triad in C major or C minor is C;
- the root of a subdominant triad in C major or C minor is F;
- the root of a dominant triad in C major or C minor is G.

The tonic, subdominant and dominant triads are the **primary triads** of a key. In major keys, all three triads are 'major triads' because they all contain an interval of a major 3rd above the root. In minor keys the dominant triad is also a *major* triad. However, in minor keys the tonic and subdominant triads are 'minor triads', because they both contain an interval of a minor 3rd above the root.

The roman numerals I, IV and V are often used as 'shorthand' signs for the tonic, subdominant and dominant triads respectively, for example (in C major):

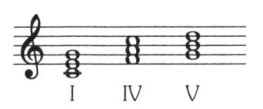

[Musical notation: treble clef, C major, three triads labeled:]
I   IV   V

You may find these shorthand signs useful in your own work, but you will not be required to use them in the Grade 4 examination: you will be able to use just words if you prefer.

Originally, the roman numerals were always written as capital letters, and did not indicate whether the triads were major or minor. But a useful development has been to use capital letters for major triads only, and small ('lower case') letters for minor triads, for example (in C minor):

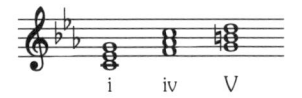

(musical example: C minor triads labelled i, iv, V)

This later method — known as 'extended roman'[1] — is used in the present book, although you should note that it is not used in Grades 1 to 5 of *Music Theory in Practice*. If you do wish to use roman figures in the examination, either method will be acceptable: you will not be penalised for using capital letters only. Here is a list of the primary triads in all the keys set for Grade 4:

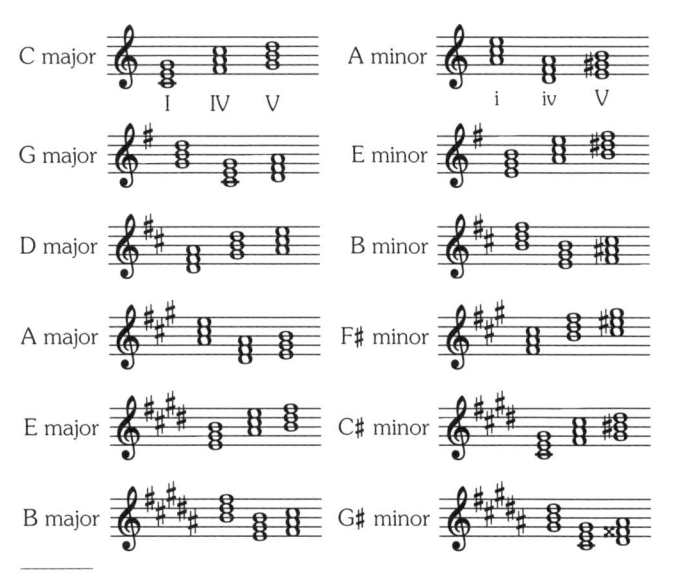

(musical examples: primary triads I, IV, V in C major, G major, D major, A major, E major, B major; and i, iv, V in A minor, E minor, B minor, F♯ minor, C♯ minor, G♯ minor)

---

[1] See Appendix D in Part II of *The AB Guide to Music Theory*.

F major Bb major Eb major Ab major Db major

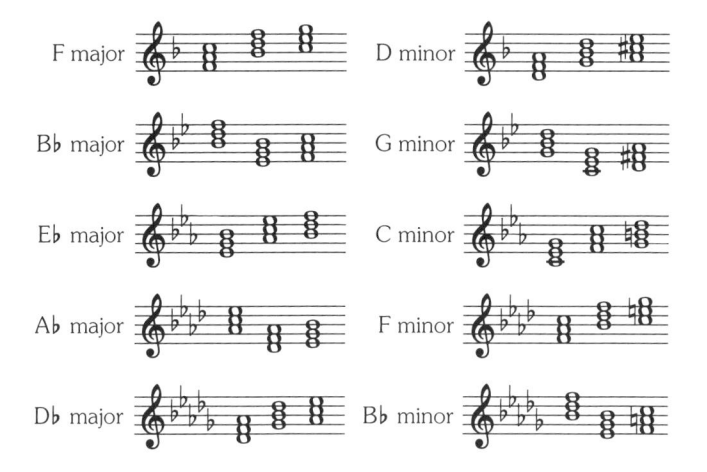

D minor G minor C minor F minor Bb minor

11 Chords on the Tonic, Subdominant and Dominant

A chord is a group of three or more notes which are played or sung together. In conventional harmony the basic chords consist of notes belonging to a triad. A triad is, in fact, the simplest type of chord. However, it is also a special type, because in a chord:

- the notes may be used more than once, at any number of octaves higher or lower; and
- the notes are usually spaced out, with gaps between them.

These, for instance, are all chords made from the tonic triad of C major:

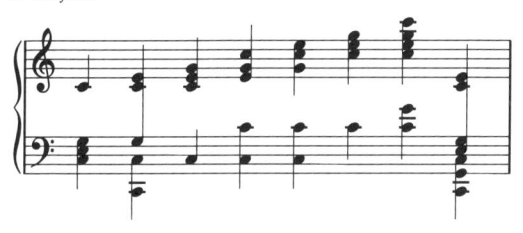

Because the bottom note (the 'bass note') of each of these chords is the root of the triad they are all said to be 'in root position'.

In Grade 4 you will not be asked to *write* chords, but you may be asked to *name* certain chords in a few bars of music. The chords will be tonic, dominant or subdominant chords only; and they will always be in root position. All you need to know, therefore, is the key, and which degree of its scale the bottom note of the chord is on. In this passage, for instance, the key is E minor:

- The bottom note of the chord marked 1 is A, the 4th degree of the scale of E minor, so the chord is a subdominant chord (iv).
- The bottom note of the chord marked 2 is B, the 5th degree of the scale of E minor, so the chord is a dominant chord (V).

Here is another example, this time in A♭ major:

- The bottom note of the chord marked 1 is A♭, the 1st degree of the scale of A♭ major, so the chord is a tonic chord (I).
- The bottom note of the chord marked 2 is D♭, the 4th degree of the scale of A♭ major, so the chord is a subdominant chord (IV).

- The bottom note of the chord marked 3 is A♭, so this is another tonic chord (I).

Again, if you wish to indicate chords by roman numerals in the examination you may do so, but you will not be *required* to do so; and if you *do* use them you will not be penalised for using capital letters only.

12 The Chromatic Scale

A **chromatic scale** is a scale consisting entirely of semitones. Therefore a one-octave chromatic scale contains *all* the notes within an octave, e.g.:

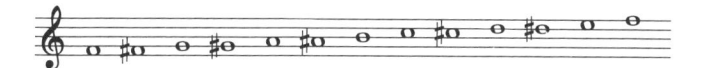

However, the same scale could be written in many different ways. This is one of them:

So the problem of writing a chromatic scale is not so much 'what are the notes?' as 'what are we to call them?'. For instance, do we write F–F♯–G–G♯–A or F–G♭–G♮–A♭–A♮?

Chromatic scales are sometimes divided into two types: the 'harmonic' chromatic scale and variable forms of the 'melodic' chromatic scale.[2] In the examination you will not be required to use either of these types. What you must remember, however, is

---

[2] See *The AB Guide to Music Theory*, Part I, 4/6.

that *there must be at least one note on every line and in every space, but not more than two*. This succession of notes is wrong, therefore, for two reasons:

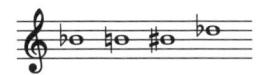

It is easier for a performer to read a chromatic scale (or a part of it) if it is written with no more accidentals than are necessary, e.g.:

is simpler than

Unnecessary accidentals can be avoided by remembering the sharps and flats in the key signature, if there is one, for example:

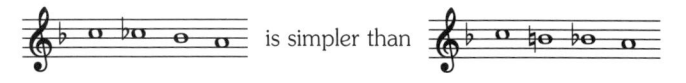

is simpler than

and

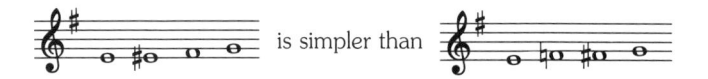

is simpler than

Also, it can be confusing when a note which is affected by the key signature is not actually used. For instance, if the first scale given in this section were to be written with an F major key signature it would be better with a B♭ instead of an A♯:

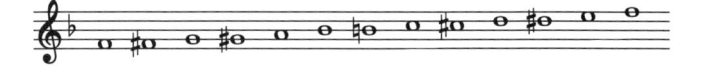

And if the same scale were written with a B♭ major key signature it would be better with an E♭ rather than a D♯:

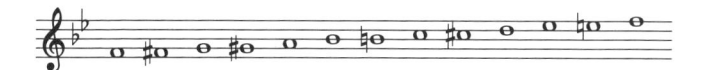

13 Ornament Signs

You may be asked to recognise and name some commonly-used 'ornament' signs which indicate various decorations of a note. The decorations are shown in two ways, either:

- by one or more small-size notes written immediately before the full-size note which they decorate: ♪, ♫, ♬, ♪, ♪ and ♩, or
- by special symbols written above the stave: *tr*, ∾, ∿ and ∞.

None of these symbols or small-size notes counts towards the number of beats in a bar: the time values of the full-size notes in a bar would be exactly the same *without* any symbols or small-size notes which may be included in it.

The names which you should use in the examination for the ornament signs are given below. (More will be said about their names in the Grade 5 section of this book, where there will also be an explanation of how the signs are interpreted.)

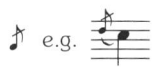

♪ e.g. (notice the diagonal stroke through the stem and flag of the small quaver): an *acciaccatura* (the Italian name) or a 'crushed' note, or a 'grace note'. Like all the following small-size notes it is often linked to the full-size note by a slur, but this is not essential.

♫ ♫♫ e.g. [music] [music] groups of two or more *acciaccature* (note the plural spelling) / crushed notes / grace notes. The number of beams has no significance.

♪ ♪ ♩ e.g. [music] [music] [music] (notice that the small quaver is without a diagonal stroke): each of these is an *appoggiatura* (plural *appoggiature*). There is no commonly-used English alternative for these Italian words.

tr (or **tr**~~~) e.g. [music] [music] a 'trill' or 'shake'

ᴡ e.g. [music] an 'upper mordent'

ᴡ e.g. [music] a 'lower mordent'

∞ e.g. [music] a 'turn'

14 The Alto Clef

As well as the G clef (𝄞) and the F clef (𝄢) there is also a C clef. It is printed thus: 𝄡. (The two upright lines at the left are not bar lines; they are part of the clef.) When the C clef is centred on the *middle* line of the stave it is called the **alto clef**,[3] and the middle line then represents middle C:

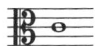

Therefore these three examples all sound exactly the same, even though they are written in different clefs:

In the alto clef, the key signatures of the keys you have studied so far are arranged like this:

The only instrument which regularly uses the alto clef now is the viola, but in earlier times it was more widely used, particularly in vocal music.

---

[3] We shall see in the next Grade that a C clef can also be centred on the *4th* line, and is then known as the 'tenor clef'.

15 General Questions

You may have to answer some simple questions requiring a little knowledge of standard orchestral instruments. Orchestral instruments are divided into four main groups: string, woodwind, brass and percussion instruments. The standard string, woodwind and brass instruments are listed below. In each column, the instrument which can produce the highest notes is at the top, and the instrument which produces the deepest notes is at the bottom. When a clef is underlined it means that the instrument's music is always written in this clef. Clefs which are *not* underlined are the clefs which the instruments *normally* use, but others may be used instead if the music goes particularly high or low.

Strings	**Woodwind**	**Brass**
violin (<u>treble clef</u>)	flute (<u>treble clef</u>)	trumpet (<u>treble clef</u>)
viola (alto clef)	oboe (<u>treble clef</u>)	horn (treble clef)
cello (bass clef)	clarinet (<u>treble clef</u>)	trombone (bass clef)
double bass (bass clef)	bassoon (bass clef)	tuba (<u>bass clef</u>)

String and brass instruments may use mutes — devices which soften the sound. The direction *con sordini* (or *con sord.*) means 'with mutes'; *senza sordini* (or *senza sord.*) means 'without mutes'. *Pizzicato* (or *pizz.*) is a direction to string players to pluck the strings with the fingers instead of playing them with the bow; *arco* means that the bow is to be used again. In string music the signs ⊓ and ⋁ are bowing marks, indicating a 'down' bow and an 'up' bow respectively. A slur over or under two or more notes (⌒ or ⌣) means that they are to be played in a single bow-stroke, either up or down. *Sul G* means play 'on the G string' and *sul ponticello* means play 'near the bridge'.

Traditionally, the standard percussion instruments in the orchestra are timpani ('kettle drums'), the side drum, bass drum and cymbals.[4] Of these, only the timpani produce notes of definite pitch: thus at least two of them are included, tuned to different notes (e.g. the tonic and dominant).

Below is a list of Italian and French words and their meanings which you should know in Grade 4. (It is the same as the list printed in *Music Theory in Practice*, Grade 4.)

affettuoso	tenderly
affrettando	hurrying
amabile	amiable, pleasant
appassionato	with passion
calando	getting softer, dying away (and usually slowing down)
cantando	singing
come	as, similar to (*come prima*: as before; *come sopra*: as above)
facile	easy
fuoco	fire
giusto	proper, exact (*tempo giusto*: in strict time)
l'istesso	the same (*l'istesso tempo*: at the same speed)
morendo	dying away
niente	nothing
nobilmente	nobly
perdendosi	dying away
possibile	possible (*presto possibile*: as fast as possible)
quasi	as if, resembling
sonoro	resonant, with rich tone
sopra	above
sotto	below (*sotto voce*: in an undertone)

---

[4] Many others, of course, may also be required, including some which are often used in school music classes, such as the triangle and the xylophone.

veloce	swift
voce	voice
à	to, at
animé	animated, lively
assez	enough, sufficiently
avec	with
cédez	yield, relax the speed
douce	sweet
en dehors	prominent (a direction to make a melody stand out)
et	and
légèrement	light
lent	slow
mais	but
moins	less
modéré	at a moderate speed
non	not
peu	little
plus	more
presser	hurry (*en pressant*: hurrying on)
ralentir	slow down
retenu	held back (*en retenant*: holding back, slowing a little)
sans	without
très	very
un, une	one
vif	lively
vite	quick

Grade 5

1 Irregular Time Signatures

Time signatures which do not indicate duple, triple or quadruple time (either simple or compound) are described as 'irregular'. The most common examples indicate five beats in a bar (quintuple time) or seven beats (septuple time). In Grade 5, the only irregular time signatures used will be $\frac{5}{4}$, $\frac{7}{4}$, $\frac{5}{8}$ and $\frac{7}{8}$.

Bars with an irregular time signature are almost always combinations of two- (or four-) and three-beat groups. Here are two examples:

(3+2 crotchets)

(4+3 quavers)

There are no special 'rules' about the grouping of notes and rests: each subdivision of an irregular bar is grouped in the usual way, i.e. just as it would be if it were a complete two-, three- or four-beat bar. In the last bar of the $\frac{7}{8}$ example above, for instance, the tied notes follow the 4+3 pattern established in the previous bars, and therefore are *not* written

2 Irregular Time Divisions

The simplest irregular time division is a triplet — a group of three equal notes performed in the time normally taken by two of them, e.g.:

♪♪♪ (3) performed in the time of ♪♪ (= ♩)

Other irregular time divisions which you may meet are:

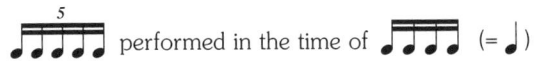

5 performed in the time of 4, e.g.:

♪♪♪♪♪ (5) performed in the time of ♪♪♪♪ (= ♩)

6 performed in the time of 4, e.g.:

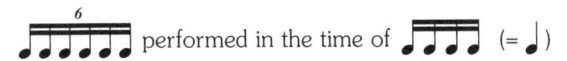

♪♪♪♪♪♪ (6) performed in the time of ♪♪♪♪ (= ♩)

7 performed in the time of 4, e.g.:

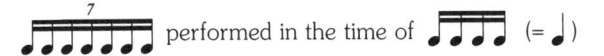

♪♪♪♪♪♪♪ (7) performed in the time of ♪♪♪♪ (= ♩)

9 performed in the time of 8, e.g.:

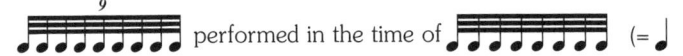

♪♪♪♪♪♪♪♪♪ (9) performed in the time of ♪♪♪♪♪♪♪♪ (= ♩)

Notice that:
- 5, 6 or 7 notes in the time of a crotchet are written as semiquavers (i.e. with two beams), but
- 9 notes in the time of a crotchet are written as demisemiquavers (i.e. with three beams).

Here are two examples:

When an irregular group is performed in the time of a note other than a crotchet (e.g. a quaver or a minim) its time values are adjusted accordingly. For example:
- 5, 6 or 7 notes in the time of a quaver are written as demisemiquavers,
- 9 notes in the time of a minim are written as semiquavers.

Compare these two examples with the two above:

3 The Tenor Clef; Octave Transpositions

The **tenor clef** is another C clef, like the alto clef. The difference between them is that the tenor clef is centred on the *fourth* line, so it is the *fourth* line which represents middle C:

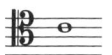

Because the alto and tenor clefs are so similar it is particularly important to draw them carefully, and to notice which is which in a printed piece of music. Here the same melody is written out for each of them, and for the bass clef, with all three at exactly the same pitch:

We have now met all the clefs which are still in regular use. Note that the treble clef has the highest range of notes; the alto clef a rather lower range; the tenor clef a lower range still; while the bass clef has the lowest range of all. The tenor clef can be used by cellos, bassoons and tenor trombones (although all of them also use the bass clef). It is no longer used by *singers*, as we shall see in Section 13.

You may be asked to transpose a melodic passage an octave higher or lower, using a different clef. There was a similar exercise in Grade 3, but only the treble and bass clefs were used there. In Grade 5 *any* of the four clefs may be required. This is not a difficult exercise, but two mistakes are quite common. One is to use the wrong C clef — to use the alto instead of the tenor clef, or vice versa. The other is to write the melody at the wrong pitch (usually at the *same* pitch, but sometimes two octaves higher or lower). For instance, if the question asks you to 'transpose this melody an octave lower, using the treble clef':

the answer is

not ... (same pitch).

Similarly, if the question asks you to 'transpose this melody an octave higher, using the tenor clef':

the answer is

not ... (same pitch)

and not ... (wrong clef).

4 The Scales of F Sharp Major and D Sharp Minor

In Grade 5 the new scales are those with six sharps or six flats:
- F♯ major and its relative minor, D♯ minor;
- G♭ major and its relative minor, E♭ minor.

These two pairs of scales are enharmonic equivalents of each other: on a keyboard the notes of the scale of F♯ major are exactly the same as those of G♭ major. So the notes of each of the D♯ minor scales (harmonic and melodic) are the same as those of the scales of E♭ minor.

The scales of the sharp keys are given below, and those of the flat keys will follow in the next Section. You will not be asked to write out scales in the alto and tenor clefs, but you should know the layout of the key signatures in all clefs. Notice now how they are arranged in the sharp keys:

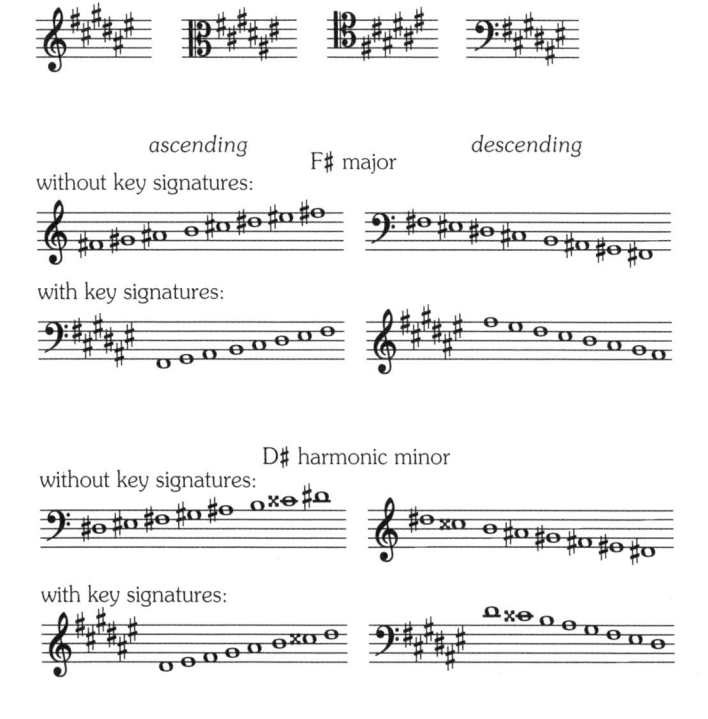

F♯ major

ascending   *descending*

without key signatures:

with key signatures:

D♯ harmonic minor

without key signatures:

with key signatures:

D♯ melodic minor

without key signatures:

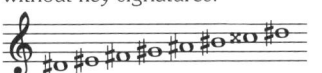

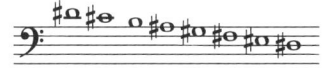

with key signatures:

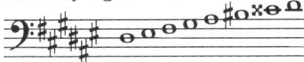

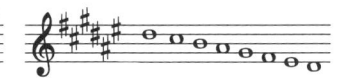

5 The Scales of G Flat Major and E Flat Minor

This is how key signatures of six flats are laid out:

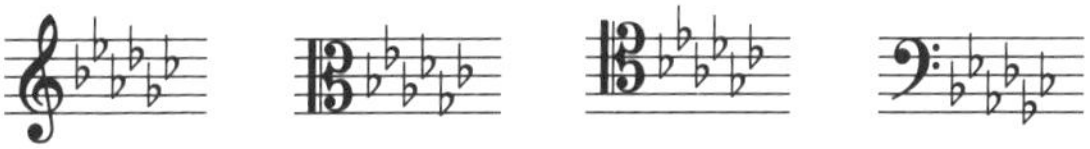

Here are the scales:

ascending *descending*

G♭ major

without key signatures:

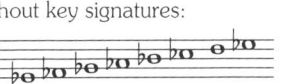

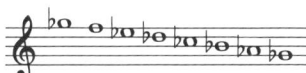

with key signatures:

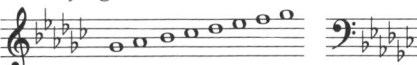

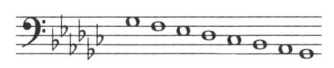

E♭ harmonic minor

without key signatures:

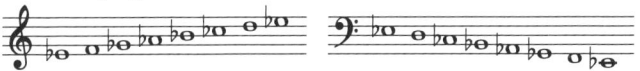

with key signatures:

without key signatures: E♭ melodic minor

6 Diatonic and Chromatic Intervals

A **diatonic interval** is an interval between two notes which both occur in the same diatonic (major or minor) scale. The intervals explained in Grade 4 were all diatonic intervals. An interval between two notes which do *not* occur in the same diatonic scale is a **chromatic interval**. Here is an example:

No diatonic scale contains both A♭ and F♯, so this is a chromatic interval.

Most chromatic intervals can be named in the same way that intervals were named in Grade 4 (see Section 9). For instance, if the above interval had been

it would have been a major 6th, but the interval becomes a semitone larger when the F is changed to F♯, so A♭ to F♯ is an *augmented* 6th. Similarly,

is a minor 6th, but

is a semitone *smaller*, so C♯ to A♭ is a *diminished* 6th.

The interval between two notes which are a semitone apart may be diatonic or chromatic.

is a diatonic interval — a minor 2nd — because both notes can be found in one scale (e.g. A♭ major or D♭ major). It can also be described as a 'diatonic semitone'. Its enharmonic equivalent

is a chromatic interval because there is no diatonic scale which includes both C♮ and C♯. It would most commonly be called a 'chromatic semitone', although it may also be described as an 'augmented 1st'. (Note that it cannot be a 2nd of any kind because both notes have the same letter name.)

Any chromatic intervals which you are asked to name in the Grade 5 examination will be intervals which can be named in the ways described above. Elsewhere you may come across intervals which cannot be named in *any* of these ways, for instance, the last of these three intervals:

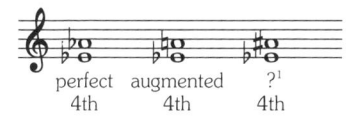

perfect augmented ?[1]
4th   4th   4th

---

[1] It is a 'doubly-augmented 4th', but not every possibility can be covered even by the word 'doubly'!

7 Compound Intervals

So far, the intervals which we have named have not been larger than an octave. Intervals of more than an octave continue to be numbered in the same way, e.g.:

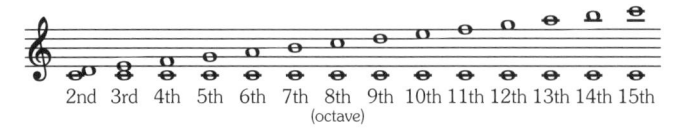

[musical example showing intervals labeled: 2nd 3rd 4th 5th 6th 7th 8th (octave) 9th 10th 11th 12th 13th 14th 15th]

However, there is a trap here. It is natural to think of, say, this interval:

as 'an octave and a 5th',

but if you then go on to add 8+5 you will get the answer 13, which is *not* the number of the interval! It is actually a 12th (i.e. 7+5), as you will understand by looking again at the first example in this Section.

There is another way of numbering intervals of more than an octave. The intervals in the higher octave keep the same numbers as the intervals in the lower octave, but add the word 'compound'. Compare, for instance:

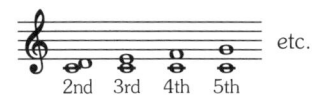

[musical example: 2nd 3rd 4th 5th] etc.

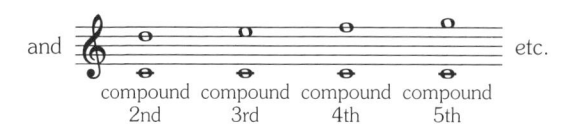

and [musical notation: compound 2nd, compound 3rd, compound 4th, compound 5th] etc.

In the examination you may give the number of an interval in either of these ways. Whichever way you choose, the *quality* of the interval remains the same, e.g.:

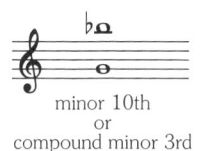

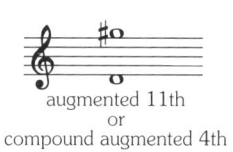

[musical notation] minor 10th or compound minor 3rd

[musical notation] augmented 11th or compound augmented 4th

8 Inversions of Triads

The triads in earlier Grades were always 'in root position'. Root-position triads are also called 'five-three' triads (written $\frac{5}{3}$) because the upper two notes are at intervals of a 5th and a 3rd above the root, e.g.:

(a) [musical notation: 5th, 3rd]

(Here, as in the examples which follow, the root of the triad is printed as a black note.)

A triad may be rearranged so that the 3rd or the 5th, not the root, is at the bottom. In these examples, triad (b) has the 3rd at the bottom and triad (c) has the 5th at the bottom:

(b) [musical notation]   (c) [musical notation]

- If the 3rd is the lowest note, a triad is 'in first inversion' — as in triad (b) above.
- If the 5th is the lowest note, a triad is 'in second inversion' — as in triad (c) above.

A first-inversion triad is also called a 'six-three' triad (written $^6_3$), because these are the intervals above its lowest note:

6th   3rd

Similarly, a second-inversion triad is a $^6_4$ triad:

6th   4th

When roman numerals are used to identify triads as tonic or dominant etc., there are two ways of showing whether a triad is in root position, first inversion or second inversion. One is to add 'a', 'b' or 'c' respectively. The other is to add the figures $^5_3$, $^6_3$ or $^6_4$; e.g. (in C major):

Ia or I$^5_3$ Ib or I$^6_3$ Ic or I$^6_4$

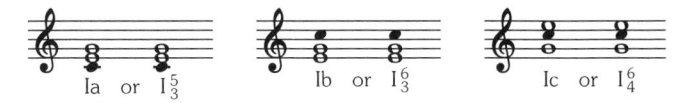

In the examination you may use either of these methods.

Chords also may be in root position, first inversion or second inversion, depending on whether the root, 3rd or 5th of the triad is the lowest note (or 'in the bass'). Compare this first inversion of a dominant triad in C minor:

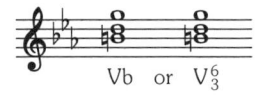

Vb or V$^6_3$

with these typical chords derived from it:

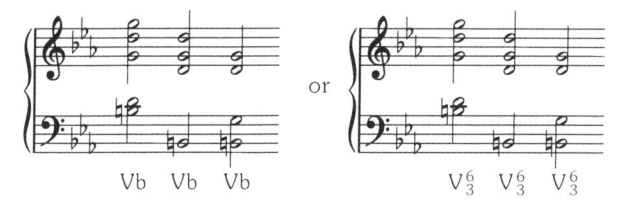

Vb Vb Vb   or   V$^6_3$ V$^6_3$ V$^6_3$

9 Identifying Chords

In Grade 5 you will be asked to identify certain chords in any of the keys set for the Grade — i.e. keys with key signatures of up to six sharps or six flats. Below is a complete list of the root-position triads whose notes these chords use. They are the triads on the tonic, supertonic, subdominant and dominant (I, II, IV and V in ordinary roman letters). In minor keys the supertonic triad is a 'diminished' triad, because the intervals above the root are a *diminished* 5th and a minor 3rd, e.g. D–A♭ in C minor:

diminished   minor
   5th   3rd

If you choose to identify chords by 'extended roman' symbols[2] (as in the top line of the examples on the following page) you should notice that a diminished triad is shown in lower-case letters followed by a tiny circle: ii°.

---

[2] See Grade 4, p. 94.

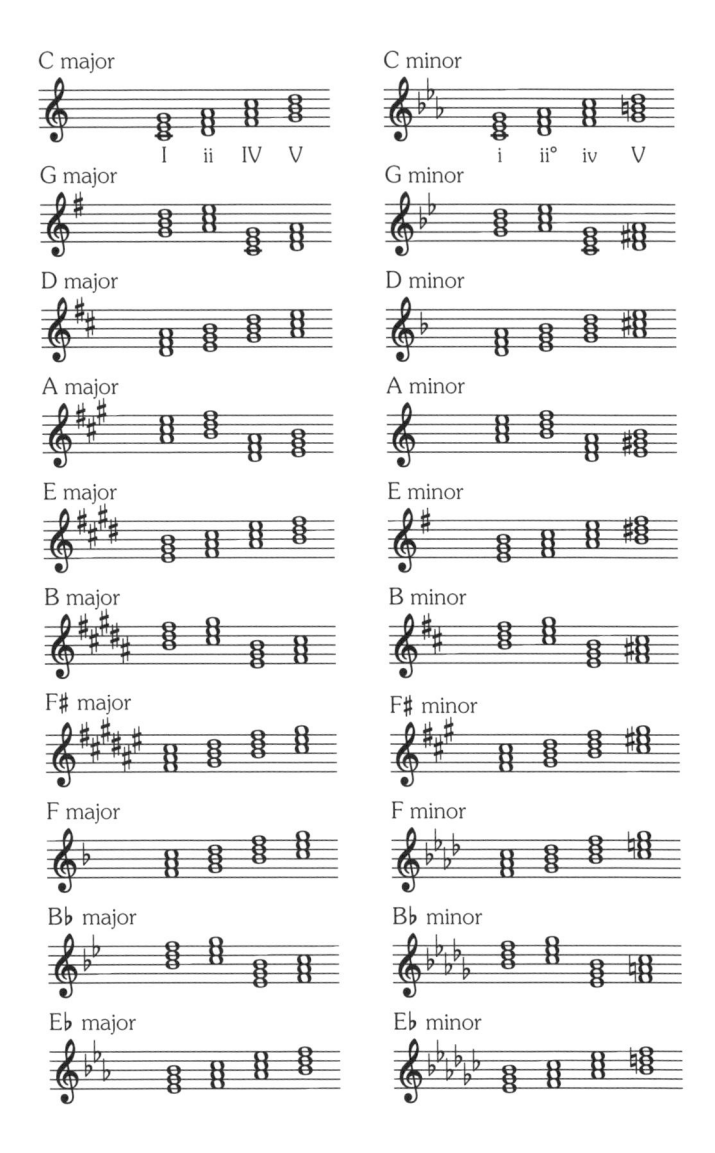

Grade 5

C major
I   ii   IV   V

C minor
i   ii°   iv   V

G major
G minor
D major
D minor
A major
A minor
E major
E minor
B major
B minor
F# major
F# minor
F major
F minor
B♭ major
B♭ minor
E♭ major
E♭ minor

A♭ major

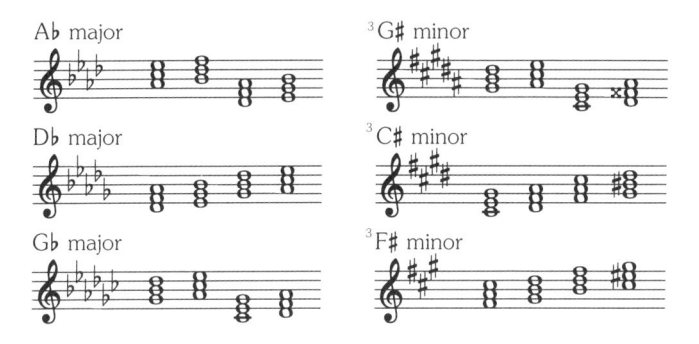

[³]G♯ minor

D♭ major

[³]C♯ minor

G♭ major

[³]F♯ minor

These are some examples of root-position chords made from the triads listed above:

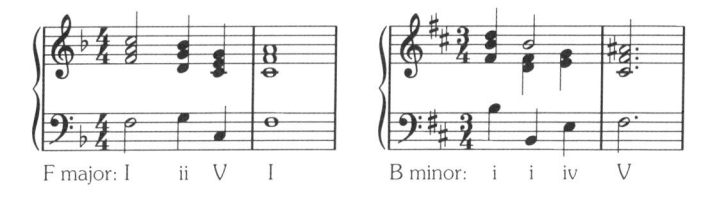

F major: I ii V I

B minor: i i iv V

E major: I IV ii V— I

---

[3] Since the minor keys of A♭, D♭ and G♭ require more than six flats, they are replaced here by their enharmonic equivalents.

Bb minor: V   i —   i   iv   i   V

In the examination you may be asked to identify inverted chords as well as root-position chords, as in these examples:

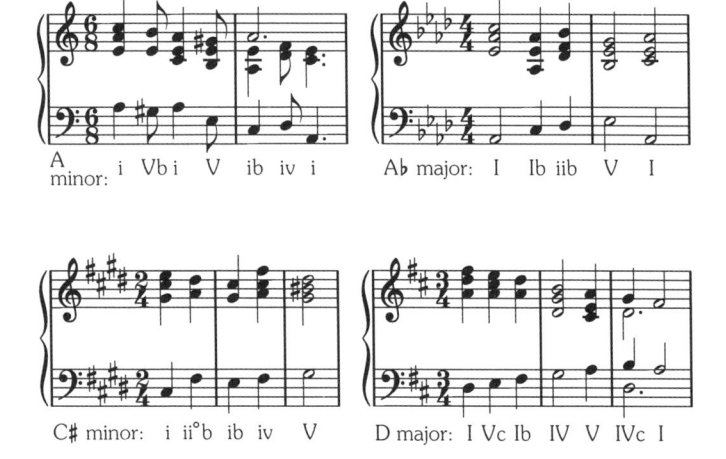

A minor: i   Vb i   V   ib iv   i

Ab major: I   Ib iib   V   I

C# minor: i   ii°b ib iv   V

D major: I   Vc Ib   IV   V   IVc I

10 The $^6_4\,^5_3$ Progression

You may also be asked to identify a particular progression of chords: a second-inversion tonic chord followed by a root-position dominant chord (Ic–V). Both of these chords have the dominant in the bass, e.g. in C major:

Musicians often refer to this progression as 'a six-four five-three', because the first chord contains intervals (or compound intervals) of a 6th and a 4th above the bass, and the second chord contains intervals (or compound intervals) of a 5th and a 3rd. In the examination you will be asked to write $\begin{smallmatrix}6\\4\end{smallmatrix}$ $\begin{smallmatrix}5\\3\end{smallmatrix}$ below the appropriate chords, as in these examples:

Mendelssohn: 'Hark, the herald angels sing'

Mozart: K236

Bear in mind that you will only be asked to identify a $^6_4$ $^5_3$ progression on the *dominant* note (as in the examples above). You will need to be careful about this because a $^6_4$ $^5_3$ progression can be used on other degrees of the scale as well as on the dominant. (See, for instance, the last two chords of the last example in Section 9, which are also a $^6_4$ $^5_3$ progression, but with the bass notes on the tonic.)

11 Chords at Cadence Points

Cadence points in music can be compared to places where there are punctuation marks in prose or poetry. Just as a full stop is used when a statement has been completed, so a cadence point marks the end of a stage in music. Some cadence points are more important than others — similar to the way in which a sentence may be divided into sections separated by commas.

In music, a cadence is produced by a combination of features: the rhythm, the rise and fall of the melody, and the use of particular chord progressions. However, in Grade 5 the cadence points will be indicated. All you will be asked to do is to suggest suitable chords for them. The cadence points will occur in a simple melody in one of these major keys: C, G, D or F.

A cadence requires two *different* chords, and you will need to know the pairs of chords which are regularly used. At this Grade, they can be divided into two main groups:
- cadences which end on a tonic chord, and
- cadences which end on a dominant chord.

There are two cadences which end on a tonic chord. By far the more common of the two is the 'perfect' cadence: a dominant chord followed by a tonic chord (V–I), e.g.:

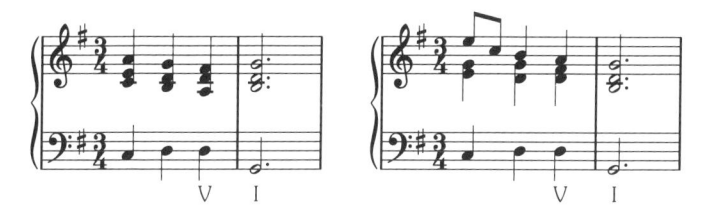

The other is a 'plagal' cadence: a subdominant chord followed by a tonic chord (IV–I), e.g.:

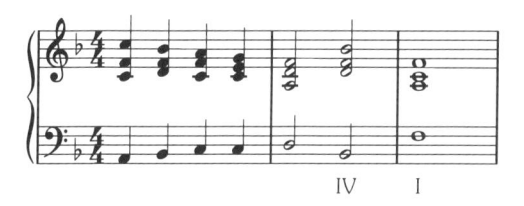

Cadences which end on the dominant are all called 'imperfect' cadences. There are several chords which *can* be used before the dominant chord, but in the examination you will need to use only I–V, ii–V or IV–V, e.g.:

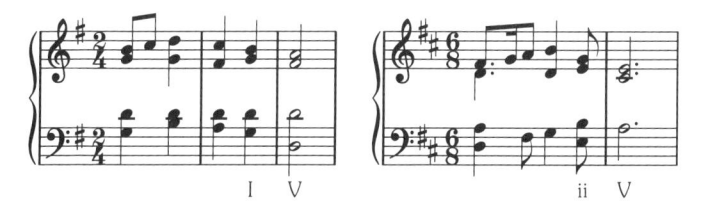

[music example with chords IV V]

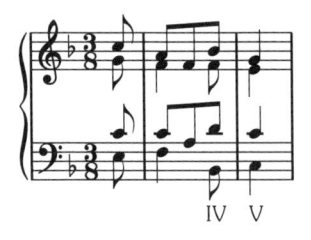

In the examination you may also be asked to choose a chord to go *before* two cadence chords, thereby making a progression of three chords. A chord before two cadence chords is referred to as an 'approach' chord. The chords marked * here are examples:

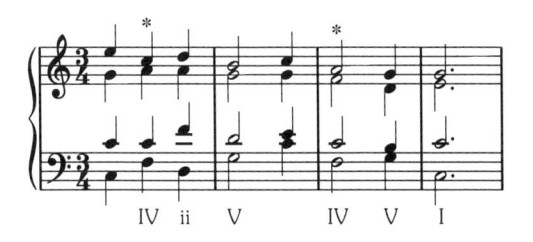

[music example with chords IV ii V | IV V I]

Again, it will always be possible to choose a suitable approach chord from chords I, ii, IV or V.

The melody notes requiring chords will be marked A, B, C etc. The only approach chord which is asked for in this example is chord C:

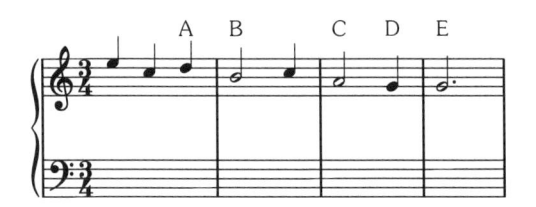

[music example with melody notes labelled A B C D E]

You may indicate the chords in any one of these ways:
- by roman numerals, e.g. Chord A: ii; Chord B: V;
- by the letter names of their notes, e.g. Chord A: d-f-a; Chord B: g-b-d;
- by writing notes on the staves. If you are studying harmony, you may prefer to write notes on the staves in ways you are used to, e.g.:

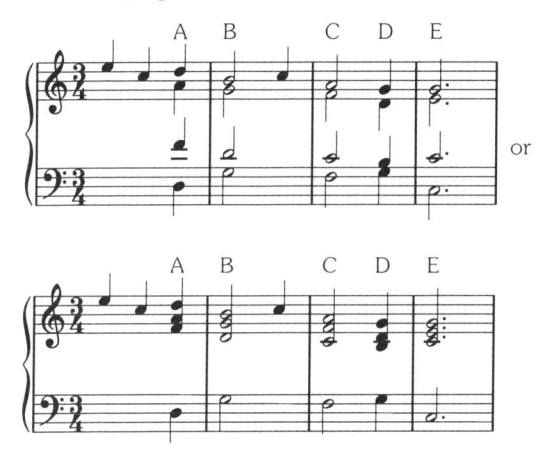

or

However, this is not meant to be a full-scale exercise in harmonisation, and you will not be penalised for poor spacing, or for faults in part-writing etc. All that is being tested is your understanding of the basic chords which might be appropriate at particular points. At their very simplest the chords can be represented by root-position triads, e.g.:

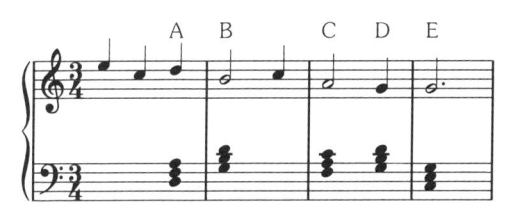

You may well find that a letter (A, B, C etc.) applies to two notes, e.g.:

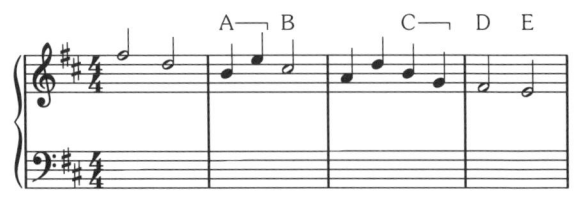

When this happens, *both* notes are to be harmonised by the same chord. In this last example, chord A must be ii, because ii is the only chord in D major which includes both e and b. But chord C could be either ii (e-g-b) or IV (g-b-d).

If you choose to indicate the chords by the letter names of their notes, remember to mention any sharps or flats which are caused by the key signature. For instance, chord B in the last example would be 'a – c$\sharp$ – e'.

12 Transposition by Instruments in B Flat, A and F

Some instruments produce sounds which are lower or higher than those indicated by the written notes. A simple example is the double bass, the deepest instrument in the string section of the orchestra, whose notes always sound an octave *lower* than the written notes. Another example is the piccolo (a small version of the flute), whose notes always sound an octave *higher* than the written notes.

Other instruments produce notes which sound at other intervals below or above the written notes. The most common are:
- instruments whose notes sound *a tone lower* than the written notes. These are instruments 'in B♭', because when they play a written C they actually sound B♭, e.g. clarinets in B♭ and trumpets in B♭;

- instruments whose notes sound *a minor 3rd lower* than the written notes. These are instruments 'in A', because when they play a written C they actually sound A, e.g. clarinets in A and trumpets in A;
- instruments whose notes sound *a perfect 5th lower* than the written notes. These are instruments 'in F', because when they play a written C they actually sound F, e.g. horns (= French horns) in F and the cor anglais.

The music *written* for these instruments has to be transposed if it is to sound at the right pitch. For instance, if a piece in G major is played by a clarinet in B♭ and a piano, the piano part will be written in G but the clarinet part will be written a tone higher (in A major). Thus, if this phrase for the piano

is to be repeated by the clarinet, it will have to be written as

in the clarinet part.

To prevent misunderstandings, musicians make a distinction between the written pitch of a note and what they call its 'concert' pitch — the pitch at which it actually sounds. The first note of the clarinet part above could be called either 'written E' or 'concert D' (or 'D concert').

In the examination you will be asked to transpose a short melody for an instrument in B♭, A or F, either from its written pitch to its concert pitch or the other way round. What this means in effect is that you will be asked to transpose a melody in one of these ways:

up a tone	(from concert to written pitch for an instrument in B♭) or
down a tone	(from written to concert pitch for an instrument in B♭);
up a minor 3rd	(from concert to written pitch for an instrument in A) or
down a minor 3rd	(from written to concert pitch for an instrument in A);
up a perfect 5th	(from concert to written pitch for an instrument in F) or
down a perfect 5th	(from written to concert pitch for an instrument in F).

The question will tell you which of these intervals is required. For example, you may be given a melody in D major, and asked to transpose it up a minor 3rd, as it would be written for a clarinet in A. Your first task is to work out the new key. The minor 3rd above D is F, so the new key is F major. Next you write in the new key signature (one flat), and then write out all the notes a 3rd higher. But do not assume that any accidentals in the D major melody will remain the same in F major. For example, G♯ is an augmented 4th above the keynote in D; but the augmented 4th above the keynote in F is B♮. Similarly a G♮ in D major would become a B♭ in F major. So if the D major melody begins

the transposed version will begin

Notice, too, that the B♮ in the last example should *not* be written as C♭ (its enharmonic equivalent):

C♭ is a diminished 5th above the keynote, not the augmented 4th it should be.

Remember to include any performance directions (tempo, phrasing etc.) which are given in the original — just as you would need to do if you were transposing it for use in an actual performance.

13 SATB in Short and Open Score

The most common combination of voices in a choir or chorus is sopranos (or trebles), altos, tenors and basses: SATB for short. Music for these voices is very often written on two staves, with the soprano and alto parts on the upper stave and the tenor and bass parts on the lower stave. The stems of the soprano and tenor notes always go up, and the stems of the alto and bass notes always go down, e.g.:

If the chord had been written like this:

it would mean that the *altos* are to sing the B on the treble stave and the sopranos are to sing the G. A note on a stave which is sung by both voices is written with two stems, one up and one down:

If the note is a semibreve it may be written as two overlapping semibreves, or two written side by side:

When the four voice parts are combined on two staves, the music is said to be written 'in short score'. But if each voice part has a stave of its own, the music is 'in open score'. Here is the first chord in this Section written in open score:

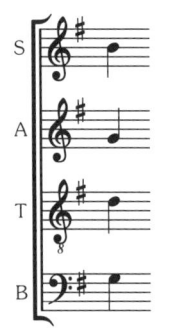

You can see from this example that an important difference between vocal music in short score and vocal music in open score is the way the tenor part is written. In short score it is written in the bass clef and at its actual (concert) pitch. In open score it is written in a *treble* clef, an octave higher than it sounds. Actually, the '8' below the treble clef is a sign that the part is to be sung an octave lower, e.g.:

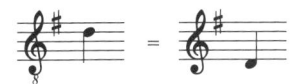

But this is a fairly recent innovation, and you will not find the 8 in older music.

In the examination you will be asked to transcribe a passage in short score into open score, or the other way round. For instance, you could be given either of the passages below and asked to transcribe it into the other. Whichever you have to do, make sure that the notes are properly aligned — in other words, that a note which should be directly underneath another note *is* directly underneath. If you are writing in open score, put in the 8 below the treble clef for the tenor. Each stave usually has separate bar lines, both in short score (below) and in open score (on the following page).

Blow: Ode for St Cecilia's Day, 1691

14 Ornaments

We saw in Grade 4 that ornament signs may be written as small-size notes (e.g. ♪) or as symbols (e.g. ∞). Whichever way they are written, the time taken to perform them has to come from the ordinary (full-size) notes. This can make it difficult to write down the *exact* rhythm of an ornament, and in Grade 5 you will not be asked to do so. But you should know what each sign represents, and you may be asked to replace written-out ornaments by notes with the appropriate ornament signs.

Below is a brief explanation of the signs listed in Grade 4 (pp. 99–100). It is important to understand, however, that there is rarely only one 'correct' way of interpreting an ornament sign. Many things may have to be taken into account: for instance, the tempo, style and mood of the music, and the period in which it was composed. And even then much may be left to the discretion and taste of the individual performer.

☆ ☆ ☆

♪ The *acciaccatura* or 'crushed note' is played as quickly as possible before the main note (the large-size note which follows it). Depending on the circumstances, it may take its time from the main note itself or from the note before it; but in either case the main note takes the accent, e.g.:

[musical example] might be performed as

[musical example] or as

[musical example]

On a keyboard instrument an acciaccatura may even be played *simultaneously* with the main note, and then released immediately:

[musical example]

☆ ☆ ☆

♪ or ♪ or ♩ The first of these *appoggiatura* signs (♪) is dangerously similar to the sign for an acciaccatura (♪), but the two have very different meanings. An appoggiatura is a note above or below the main note, but unlike an acciaccatura it has a measurable time value. Also, an appoggiatura is always more strongly accented than the main note. Indeed, it pushes the main note on to a weaker beat, or a weaker part of the beat. An appoggiatura can therefore be said to 'lean against' the main note — which is what the Italian word literally means.

Generally an appoggiatura takes *half* the value of the main note if the main note is undotted, e.g.:

performed

or *two thirds* of the value if the main note is dotted, e.g.:

performed

It cannot be assumed that the time value in which the appoggiatura is written is a safe guide to how long it should last in performance. The last example above, for instance, would still be performed in the same way if the appoggiatura were written:

And it has to be said that not all composers have used small-sized notes (including ♪) consistently, or in the ways outlined above.[4]

☆ ☆ ☆

---

[4] See *The AB Guide to Music Theory*, Part I, Ch. 12.

tr or ***tr***⌇⌇ A 'trill' or 'shake' sign indicates that the written note is to alternate rapidly with the note *above* it, e.g. [notation] etc. The trill commonly ends with a 'closing pattern' involving the use of the note *below* the last main note. These last two notes may be written in as a pair of grace notes, e.g.:

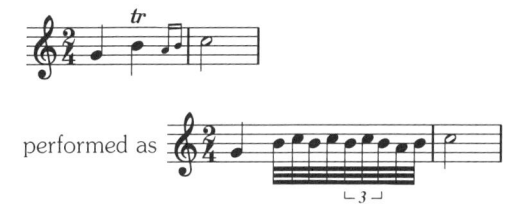

performed as [notation]

but the pattern is performed in the same way even if the grace notes are not shown. Until the early part of the 19th century, a trill normally began on the upper note, e.g.:

performed as [notation]

The number of notes in a trill depends on the speed of the music: a trill in a slow tempo will need more notes (and therefore shorter time values) than one in a quick tempo. Compare, for instance:

Moderato

performed as [notation] and

Presto

[musical example: Presto, 2/4, with trill (tr) ornament]

performed as [musical example showing realization with triplet]

☆ ☆ ☆

⚬ ⚬ During the 19th century these two ornament signs came to mean simply a rapid alternation of the written note with either the note *above* it (⚬) or the note *below* it (⚬), e.g.:

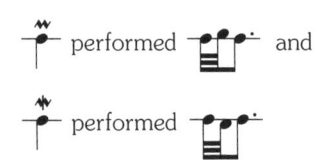

[ornament example] performed [realization] and

[ornament example] performed [realization]

Strictly speaking, the *lower* form, ⚬ , is a **mordent** (without qualification); but this name has often been applied to the upper form, ⚬ . To prevent misunderstanding, the two ornaments are now generally distinguished as 'upper' and 'lower' mordents.

In the time of Bach and Handel, the ⚬ sign usually meant a decoration beginning with the note above the written note, followed by one or more alternations, e.g.:

[ornament example] performed [realization] or [realization]

This type of ornament was in fact a short trill or shake, and could be indicated by any of the signs ⚬ , ⚬ or *tr* . The lower form ⚬ — the true 'mordent' (*Mordant* in German) — began with the written note itself, but could also be followed by one or more alternations, e.g.: [ornament example] performed [realization] or [realization]

☆ ☆ ☆

- The 'turn' symbol represents a group of notes consisting of:
  the note *above* the written note;
  the written note;
  the note *below* the written note;
  the written note again; i.e. ∽ performed ♪♪♪♪

In the examples below, the four notes of the turn group are marked ⌐⌐.

A turn's rhythmical interpretation depends on whether the symbol is placed *directly* over a note or further to the right. It can also depend on the speed of the music. For example, a turn directly over a note, e.g.:

always begins immediately, but it might be performed

at a medium or slow tempo, or

at a fast tempo. If the turn is to the right of the written note it always begins after the written note has been sounded, and then leads straight into the next written note. For instance:

might be performed

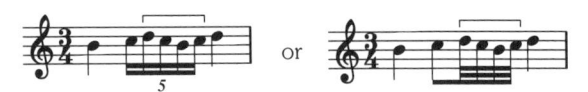

[musical notation] or *[musical notation]*

When the turn comes after a *dotted* note, e.g.:

[musical notation]

the last note of the turn is always given the time value represented by the dot, in this instance the last B:

[musical notation]

Notice that the first three notes of a turn group are always equal in value, but the time value of the fourth note is variable.

If you have to draw a turn symbol, make sure that you get it the right way up, because there is a very similar but different symbol called an 'inverted turn': ∾ . This is interpreted in the same ways as the ordinary turn except that it starts with the note *below* the written note, so its basic pattern becomes *[notation]* . (The inverted turn can also be represented as ⌽ — see *The AB Guide to Music Theory*, Part I, 12/2b.)

15 General Questions

Questions about a passage of music may include questions on types of voices, and on a wider range of instruments than those required in Grade 4. Below are some basic points which you should know, but there is much fuller information in Part II of *The AB Guide to Music Theory*.

Voices

We saw in Section 13 that choral music is most commonly written for voices of four different ranges: soprano (the highest), alto, tenor and bass (the deepest).[5] But singers — especially solo singers — are also classified in intermediate ranges, notably 'mezzo-soprano' (between soprano and alto) and 'baritone' (between tenor and bass).

Orchestral instruments

Strings

The harp has been a much-used instrument in the orchestra since the Romantic period and is clearly a string instrument, but nevertheless it is not regarded as a member of the *string section* of the orchestra.

Woodwind

The following additional instruments are versions of those included in Grade 4: piccolo (a smaller and therefore higher flute); cor anglais (similar to the oboe, but deeper); bass clarinet (a deeper clarinet); and double bassoon (a deeper bassoon). With the exception of the flute and piccolo, all of them are 'reed' instruments, but:

- the clarinet and bass clarinet each use a single reed, and
- the oboe, cor anglais, bassoon and double bassoon all use double reeds.

Brass

Note that the brass section in a full orchestra includes two different types of trombone: normally two 'tenor' trombones and one 'bass' (or 'tenor-bass') trombone.

---

[5] The distinctions between soprano and treble, and between alto, contralto and counter-tenor are explained in *The AB Guide to Music Theory*, Part II, Ch. 14.

Percussion

Commonly-used percussion instruments in addition to those listed in Grade 4 include (amongst others!):

- (indefinite pitch): triangle, tambourine, castanets, tam-tam (gong);
- (definite pitch): xylophone, marimba, glockenspiel, vibraphone, celesta, tubular bells.

Non-orchestral instruments

Some of the most widely-used instruments are not regular members of the standard orchestra, for example the guitar, saxophone and recorder. The piano is another example, although it very often appears as a soloist *with* an orchestra, e.g. in a concerto. Other keyboard instruments are the harpsichord, clavichord and organ. Organ music is normally written on three staves: the additional stave at the bottom is for the notes played on the pedal-board.

The following directions refer to the use of the pedals in piano music:

una corda	(literally 'one string') press the left pedal
tre corde	(literally 'three strings') release the left pedal
𝄢. ✻ or *P*_____	press...release the right pedal

Note these directions as well:

mano sinistra, *m.s.*	left hand
mano destra, *m.d.*	right hand
⦃	spread the notes of the chord quickly, starting from the bottom note

In Grade 5 you should understand the signs used to show reiterations and repeats (see Chapter 13 in *The AB Guide to Music Theory*), and you will also be expected to know the meaning of the following Italian and German terms. (They are the same as those printed in *Music Theory in Practice*, Grade 5.)

attacca	go straight on to the next section of music
dolente	sad, mournful
dolore	grief (*doloroso*: sorrowful)
doppio movimento	twice as fast
estinto	as soft as possible, lifeless
incalzando	getting quicker
lacrimoso	sad
loco	at the normal pitch (used to cancel an *8va* direction)
lunga	long (*lunga pausa*: long pause)
lusingando	coaxing, in a sweet and persuasive style
misura	measure (*alla misura*: in strict time; *senza misura*: in free time)
ossia	or, alternatively
piacevole	pleasant
piangevole	plaintive, in the style of a lament
pochettino, *poch.*	rather little
rinforzando, *rf*, *rfz*	reinforcing
segue	go straight on
smorzando, *smorz.*	dying away in tone and speed
teneramente, *tenerezza*	tenderly, tenderness
tosto	swift, rapid (but often used in the same sense as *troppo*)
volante	flying, fast
aber	but
Ausdruck	expression
bewegt	with movement, agitated
breit	broad, expansive

ein	a, one
einfach	simple
etwas	somewhat, rather
fröhlich	cheerful, joyful
immer	always
langsam	slow
lebhaft	lively
mässig	at a moderate speed
mit	with
nicht	not
ohne	without
ruhig	peaceful
schnell	fast
sehr	very
süss	sweet
traurig	sad
und	and
voll	full
wenig	little
wieder	again
zart	tender, delicate
zu	to, too

Index

accent, 28, 50
acciaccatura (crushed note, grace note), 99, 100, 132–3
accidental, 18–19, 98–9, 128
alto clef, 101, 107–9
alto voice, 129, 139
anacrusis, *see* upbeat
appoggiatura, 100, 133–4
approach chord, 124–6
augmented interval, 90–91
    augmented 1st, 113
    augmented 4th, 91, 113, 128–9
    augmented 6th, 112
    augmented 11th, 115
    doubly augmented 4th, 113n

Bach, Johann Sebastian, 136
bar, 2–3
baritone voice, 139
bar line, 2, 7, 62, 131
bass clarinet, 139
bass clef, 5–6
bass drum, 102
bass note, 96
bassoon, 102, 108, 139
bass voice, 129
beam, 3–4, 24–5, 26, 32–3, 56, 60, 61–2
beat, 1–2, 29–30, 33–7, 53–60, 62, 105
beat pattern, 63–5
brass instruments, 102, 139
breve, 79

cadence, 122–6
cadence chords, 124
C clef, *see* alto clef, tenor clef
cello, 102, 108
choir, 129–32
chord, 95–7
chord inversion, 115–17, 120
chord progression, 120–21
chromatic interval, 112–13
chromatic scale, 97–9
chromatic semitone, 113
clarinet, 102, 126–8, 139
clef, 5–6, 7
common time, 2
compound interval, 114–15
compound time, 53, 54–60, 61–2, 80–81, 82
    compound duple time, 54, 55–8, 60
    compound quadruple time, 54–7, 58–9, 60
    compound triple time, 54–7, 58, 60
concert pitch, 127–8, 131
contralto voice, 139n
cor anglais, 127, 139
counter-tenor voice, 139n
crotchet, 1, 12, 24, 61, 106–7
    beat, 2, 34, 36
    triplet, 30–32
crushed note, *see* acciaccatura
cymbal, 103

demisemiquaver, 61–2, 106–7
diatonic interval, 112–13

diminished interval, 90–92
  diminished 5th, 92, 117, 129
  diminished 6th, 113
diminished triad, 117
dominant, 86, 87, 122
  chord, 96, 117, 120–21, 122–3
  triad, 92–3, 116
dot, 14, 25, 53, 57–9, 79–80, 138
  double dot, 79–80
double bar line, 7
double bass, 102, 126
double bassoon, 139
double flat, 83–4
double sharp, 83
double whole note, *see* breve
doubly augmented 4th, *see* augmented interval
downbeat, 63
duplet, 82
duple time, 30, 54, 60

eighth note, *see* quaver
enharmonic equivalent, 83–4, 110, 113, 129
extended roman notation, 94, 117

F clef, *see* bass clef
first inversion, 115–17
five-three triad and chord, 115–16
flag (tail), 6–7, 61
flat, 9, 18–19
flute, 102, 139

G clef, *see* treble clef
grace note, *see* acciaccatura

half note, *see* minim

Handel, George Frideric, 136
harmonic chromatic scale, 97
harmonic interval, 23, 49
harmonic minor scale, 42–3, 47
harp, 139
horn (French horn), 102, 127

imperfect cadence, 123–4
instrument, *see* brass instruments, keyboard instruments, orchestral instruments, string instruments, transposing instruments, woodwind instruments
interval, 9–11, 22–3, 43, 48–9, 73–6, 88–91, 112–13
  see also augmented interval, chromatic interval, compound interval, diatonic interval, diminished interval, harmonic interval, major interval, melodic interval, minor interval, perfect interval
inverted turn, *see* turn

key, 15, 47
keyboard, 4–5
keyboard instruments, 140
keynote, 15, 21, 22, 87
key signature, 15–17, 21–2, 42, 47–8, 110
  A♭ major, 68, 69
  A major, 39, 41
  B♭ major, 40, 41
  B♭ minor, 85, 86
  B major, 84
  B minor, 69, 70
  C minor, 71, 72, 73
  C♯ minor, 69, 71
  D♭ major, 85
  D major, 16, 17, 41

D minor, 45, 46, 47
D♯ minor, 110–11
E♭ major, 40–41
E♭ minor, 111–12
E major, 68
E minor, 44, 46, 47
F major, 17, 41, 47
F minor, 71, 72, 73
F♯ major, 110
F♯ minor, 69, 70, 71
G♭ major, 111
G major, 16, 17, 41, 47
G minor, 71, 72
G♯ minor, 84, 85

leading note, 86, 87
ledger line, 7, 38, 65–6
lower mordent, *see* mordent

Maelzel's Metronome, 28
major interval, 74, 76, 88–9, 91
  major 2nd, 92
  major 3rd, 88–9
  major 6th, 112
major scale, 19–20, 38, *see also* scale
measure, *see* bar
mediant, 86, 87
melodic chromatic scale, 97
melodic interval, 23, 49
melodic minor scale, 42–3, 47, 75
mezzo-soprano voice, 139
middle C, 8
minim, 1, 12, 24
  beat, 29, 34, 35, 36
  triplet, 31
minor interval, 74–6, 88, 91
  minor 2nd, 92, 113
  minor 3rd, 89
  minor 6th, 88
  minor 7th, 89
  minor 10th, 115
minor key, 75
minor scale, 42–3, 89, *see also* scale
mordent, 100, 136
mute, 102

natural, 9, 19
note-head, 6

oboe, 102, 139
octave, 23
  notation, 65–6
open score, 130–32
orchestral instruments, 102–3, 139–40
organ, 140
ornament, 99–100, 132–8

pause, 28
percussion instruments, 102–3, 140
perfect cadence, 123
perfect interval, 74, 88, 91
  perfect 4th, 113
  perfect 5th, 88, 89
  perfect 12th, 114
performance directions, 27–8, 49–51, 76–7, 103–4, 141–2
piano, 140
piccolo, 126, 139
pitch, 13
plagal cadence, 123
primary triads, 93–5

quadruple time, 30, 55, 58–9, 60
quarter note, *see* crotchet
quaver, 3, 12, 24, 61
  beat, 29, 34, 36

quintuplet, 106–7
quintuple time, 105

relative major key, 47
  A minor, 47
  B♭ minor, 84
  B minor, 69
  C minor, 71
  C♯ minor, 69
  D minor, 47
  D♯/E♭ minor, 109
  E minor, 47
  F minor, 71
  F♯ minor, 69
  G minor, 71
  G♯ minor, 84
relative minor key, 47
  A♭ major, 71
  A major, 69
  B♭ major, 71
  B major, 84
  C major, 47
  D♭ major, 84
  D major, 69
  E♭ major, 71
  E major, 69
  F major, 47
  F♯/G♭ major, 109
  G major, 47
repeat mark, 28
rest, 12–13, 33–7, 57–60, 62, 80
roman numeral notation, 93–4, 116, *see also* extended roman notation
root, 93
root position, 96, 115, 119–20

scale, 10–12, 15, 19–20, 47
  A♭ major, 68, 69
  A major, 38–9
  A minor, 42–3, 44, 45
  B♭ major, 39–40
  B♭ minor, 86
  B major, 84
  B minor, 70
  C major, 10–11, 15–16, 20–21, 75
  C minor, 73, 75
  C♯ minor, 71
  D♭ major, 85
  D major, 11, 15, 16, 20
  D minor, 45, 46
  D♯ minor, 110–11
  E♭ major, 40–41
  E♭ minor, 111–12
  E major, 68, 76
  E minor, 44, 46, 76
  F major, 12, 17, 20
  F minor, 73
  F♯ major, 110
  F♯ minor, 71
  G♭ major, 111
  G major, 16
  G minor, 72
  G♯ minor, 85
scale degree, 19–21, 22–3, 74–5, 86, 122
second inversion, 115–16, 120
semibreve, 1, 12, 33, 130
semiquaver, 3, 12, 24, 26, 61, 106–7
  triplet, 31
semitone, 9–11, 22, 97
septuplet, 106
septuple time, 105
sextuplet, 106
shake, *see* trill
sharp, 8, 18–19
short score, 130, 131
side drum, 102
simple time, 53–5, 58–60,

80–81, 82, *see also* duple time, quadruple time, triple time
six-four five-three progression, 121–2
six-four triad and chord, 115–16
sixteenth note, *see* semiquaver
six-three triad and chord, 115–17
slur, 102
soprano voice, 129, 139
staccato, 28, 50–51
stave, 5–7, 129–32, 140
stem, 6–7
string instruments, 102, 139
subdominant, 86, 87
   chord, 96, 123
   triad, 92–3, 117
submediant, 86, 88
supertonic, 86, 87
   triad, 117

tail, *see* flag
tenor clef, 101n, 107–9,
tenor voice, 129, 131
32nd note, *see* demisemiquaver
tie, 13–14, 25–6, 32, 56–7
time signature, 2–3, 7, 29–30, 53–5, 80–81
   irregular, 105
timpani, 102–3
tone (whole tone), 9–11, 22
tonic, 21, 74, 86
   chord, 96–7, 122–3
   triad, 21–2, 95–6, 117
      A♭ major, 68
      A minor, 48
      B minor, 70
      C major, 48
      C minor, 72
      C♯ minor, 70
      D major, 21–2
      D minor, 48
      E major, 68
      E minor, 48
      F major, 21, 48
      F minor, 72
      F♯ minor, 70
      G major, 21, 48
      G minor, 72
transposing instruments, 126–7
transposition, 66–7, 108–9, 126–9
treble clef, 5, 131
treble voice, 139n
triad, 92–6, 115–16
   listed, 118–19
trill (shake), 100, 135
triplet, 30–32, 54, 82, 106
triple time, 30, 54–5, 58, 60
trombone, 102, 139
trumpet, 102, 126–7
tuba, 102
turn, 100, 137–8

upbeat (anacrusis), 63–5
upper mordent, *see* mordent

viola, 101, 102
violin, 102
voices, 129–32, 139

whole note, *see* semibreve
whole tone, *see* tone
woodwind instruments, 102, 139
written pitch, 127–8